hert S.

D1590715

EXPLAINING DELINQUENCY AND DRUG USE

EXPLAINING DELINQUENCY AND DRUG USE

DELBERT S. ELLIOTT
DAVID HUIZINGA
SUZANNE S. AGETON

 **SAGE** PUBLICATIONS Beverly Hills London New Delhi

For information address:

SAGE Publications, Inc.
275 South Beverly Drive
Beverly Hills, California 90212

SAGE Publications India Pvt. Ltd. 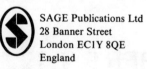 SAGE Publications Ltd
M-32 Market   28 Banner Street
Greater Kailash I   London EC1Y 8QE
New Delhi 110 048 India   England

Printed in the United States of America

Library of Congress Cataloging in Publication Data

Elliott, Delbert S.
   Explaining delinquency and drug use.

   Bibliography: p.
   1. Juvenile delinquency--United States.   2. Youth--
United States--Drug use.   3. Behavioral assessment.
I. Huizinga, David. II. Ageton, Suzanne S. III. Title.
HV9104.E445   1985   364.3'6'0973   84-24759
ISBN   0-8039-2404-6

FIRST PRINTING

CONTENTS

LIST OF FIGURES AND TABLES

Figures

Tables

ACKNOWLEDGMENTS

The National Youth Survey was initiated in June of 1975 with a five-year grant from the Center for Studies of Crime and Delinquency, National Institute of Mental Health (NIMH). The focus of the study was on the epidemiology of delinquent behavior in the American youth population and a test of a new integrated theory of delinquency (Elliott et al., 1979). The NIMH study design called for an initial survey in 1977 with a national sample of youth aged 11 through 17 in 1976 and two follow-up surveys in 1978 and 1979 with those in the original odd-aged cohorts; i.e., those who were 11-, 13-, 15-, and 17-years-old in 1976.

Prior to the 1978 survey, a second grant was obtained from the National Institute for Juvenile Justice and Delinquency Prevention (OJJDP) to study the epidemiology of drug use and the relationship between delinquency and drug use among youths in the original even-aged cohorts (12, 14, and 16). As a result, the 1978 and 1979 annual surveys were jointly funded by NIMH and OJJDP and involved the total original youth panel. The overall study is referred to as the National Youth Survey. It should be noted that the points of view and opinions expressed in this work are those of the authors and do not necessarily represent the official position or policies of the U.S. Department of Health and Human Services or the U.S. Department of Justice.

The test of the theoretical model presented here uses longitudinal data from all three surveys, providing an initial test of the model with data from the first two surveys and a replication test with data from the second and third surveys. Earlier statements of the integrated theory were admittedly incomplete and provided little empirical justification for postulated relationships (Elliott and Ageton, 1975; Elliott et al., 1979). The description of the theoretical model presented here is the most complete description and justification to date. As might be expected, our thinking underwent some modification over time, and this present statement departs in some minor respects from the earlier statements. Both Rachelle J. Canter and Brian Knowles participated in this developmental process with the authors, and we would like to acknowledge their contributions.

We would also like to acknowledge the many individuals on the National Youth Survey staff who were responsible for preparing field materials and forms, hiring and training interviewers, supervising field work, verifying completed interviews, tracking respondents, and editing, coding, and processing data for each survey. In particular we would like to recognize Catherine Bender, who was the field supervisor for each of the three annual surveys and is the person most directly responsible for the high quality of the National Youth Survey data set. Stephanie Aldridge was responsible for the preparation of the manuscript and all of the figures, tables, and graphics work.

Finally, we are indebted to the young people who participated as members of our national youth panel. Their willingness to continue participating in the study over an extended period of time and to discuss their personal involvement in illegal behavior provides the basis for this genuine predictive test of an integrated theory of delinquency.

—*Delbert S. Elliott*
—*David Huizinga*
—*Suzanne S. Ageton*

1

An Integrated Theoretical Perspective on Delinquency and Drug Use

This book presents an explanatory model that expands and synthesizes traditional strain, social control, and social learning perspectives into a single paradigm that accounts for delinquent behavior and drug use. The integration takes place at an individual level (Cohen and Short, 1976; Short, 1979), providing an explanation for how individuals become involved in delinquent acts. The dependent variable in this causal model is thus variation in individual rates of offending. No attempt is made to integrate these theoretical perspectives at the micro- or macrosociological levels although it is clear that both strain and control theories address the problem of delinquency at multiple levels of explanation (Short, 1979).

The initial formulation of this integrated theoretical perspective on the causes of delinquent behavior was presented in 1979 (Elliott et al., 1979). The model is developed more fully here, and the results of an initial test of the model with longitudinal data are presented. Although the model was initially developed as an explanation for delinquent behavior, we investigated its utility for explaining drug-using behavior as well.

The extension of the explanatory model to drug use may be justified on two grounds. First, the use of illicit drugs may be considered a specific form of delinquent behavior in that the possession of these substances involves the violation of criminal statutes and carries the risk of formal legal sanction. Although alcohol is not generally defined as an illegal substance, its use by youth under a specific age violates local and state

welfare codes and may result in police arrest and court adjudi-
cation as a delinquent youth. Second, there is considerable
empirical evidence that the use of alcohol and marijuana, the
most frequently used drugs, is part of a general deviance syndrome that involves a wide range of minor criminal acts and
other forms of norm-violating behavior (Jessor et al., 1968;
Robbins and Murphy, 1967; Hindelang and Weis, 1972; Elliott
and Ageton, 1976; Jessor and Jessor, 1977; Bachman et al.,
1978; Kandel et al., 1978; Kandel, 1980; Brennan et al., 1981;
Huizinga and Elliott, 1981; Donovan and Jessor, 1984; Elliott
and Huizinga, 1984). The presence of both delinquency and
drug use in this general syndrome suggests a common set of
causes for both types of behavior. To simplify the description
of the theoretical model and the presentation of research findings, the term delinquency will be used as a generic term that
includes illicit substance use, unless the reference is specifically
or exclusively to illicit drug use.

The successful integration of theories is a difficult task
because it nearly always involves a reconciliation of different
basic assumptions and a clarification of key theoretical concepts (Elliott, in press). The integration of these theories thus
requires some modification and extension of the "pure" forms
of these traditional theoretical perspectives. In each instance,
the extension or modification proposed is justified on both
logical and empirical grounds. In no case is the modification so
severe as to essentially deny the major causal argument(s)
intended. Rather, the pure theoretical statements are viewed as
partial explanations that are strengthened or enhanced by the
integration.

In Chapters 2 and 3, the integration of traditional strain,
social control, and social learning perspectives is described
and justified. Chapter 4 discusses the fully integrated model.
The general design of the present study, the sample, data, and
analysis plan are all described in Chapter 5. Chapter 6 presents
the results of an initial multivariate test of the integrated theoretical model and a replication of this test. In Chapter 7 we
examine the conditional relationship specified in the integrated
model in a more precise test of the model. Finally, in Chapter 8,
the implications of these findings are discussed and several
modifications of the theoretical model are proposed.

2

The Integration of Strain and Control Theories

STRAIN THEORY

Strain theory, in its simplest form, postulates that delinquency is the result of frustrated needs or wants. The earliest statements of strain theory as an explanation for delinquency viewed this frustration as resulting from a breakdown in the relationship between socially induced aspirations and socially approved ways of achieving these aspirations. Cloward and Ohlin thus hypothesized that "adolescents feel pressures for deviant behavior when they experience marked discrepancies between their aspirations and opportunities for achievement" (1960: 87). For Cloward and Ohlin (1960) and Merton (1957), this discrepancy or "strain" was experienced primarily by lower-class youths who had internalized conventional success goals but were faced with limited access to these goals because of their class positions. The primary variable influencing aspiration-opportunity discrepancies was thus differential opportunity for achieving common success goals, and strain was linked directly to the class structure.

Many lower class persons, in short, are victims of a contradiction between the goals toward which they have been led to orient themselves and socially structured means of striving for these goals. Under these conditions, there is an acute pressure to depart from institutional norms and to adopt illegitimate alternatives [Cloward and Ohlin, 1960: 105].

More recent statements of strain theory have postulated that the goal-opportunity disjunction that provides the motivation for delinquency results from variations in commitment to success goals (Simon and Gagnon, 1976) or from variations in both commitment to success goals and access to opportunities (Elliott and Voss, 1974). The significance of these new conceptualizations of the aspiration-opportunity disjunction is that they change the expected relationship between strain and social class. Simon and Gagnon (1976) argue that the disjunction described by Merton, and Cloward and Ohlin that focuses upon differential opportunities to achieve common success goals is characteristic of societies during periods of scarcity. They propose that during periods of affluence, when nearly all persons have reasonable access to opportunities for achieving success goals, it is a differential commitment to traditional success goals that generates strain and a motivation for deviance among those from higher socioeconomic levels in society. The Elliott and Voss (1974) conceptualization of strain is the most general; they postulate that middle-class youths are just as likely to aspire beyond their means as are lower-class youths. Although the absolute levels of both aspirations and opportunities may vary by class, the discrepancy between personal goals and conventional opportunities for realizing these goals need not vary systematically by class. This conceptualization of strain is thus logically independent of social class.

With the exception of the Simon and Gagnon formulation, all of these statements of strain theory assert that delinquency is a response to actual or anticipated failure to achieve socially induced needs or goals (status, wealth, power, social acceptance, etc.). Those who are unable to revise or adjust their goals in the face of this failure are forced to consider unconventional alternative means. The delinquent response is thus postulated to take one of two forms: Delinquent acts may provide for the satisfaction of these needs that could not be met by conventional, law-abiding means; or delinquent behavior may constitute an attack upon the perceived external cause of the failure or the source of the frustration (Cloward and Ohlin, 1960). In either case, the individual is motivated to violate the law because of his or her failure to satisfy personal goals or needs (which are generally encouraged and approved by the society at large) through conventional means.

CONTROL THEORY

Control theory assumes that strain is a universal state of man: All persons have frustrated wants and unfulfilled needs. This motivation to delinquency that is the critical variable in strain theories is thus a constant for control theories. The critical variable for control theorists is the strength of social controls that serve to regulate behavior and thus restrain this natural impulse to delinquency. These controls involve rewards and punishments that are expected to result from one's behavior; they may be either personal (internal) or social (external); i.e., invoked by the self or others. These rewards and punishments constitute the real or potential costs of delinquency, and it is the variability in these anticipated costs that determines one's vulnerability for delinquency.

The use of conventional or deviant means is thus dependent upon the gratification that results from these behaviors. To the extent individuals are involved in rewarding social relationships that would be jeopardized by delinquent behavior and/or anticipate personal discomfort or guilt from violating norms they believe are morally binding upon them, the costs of delinquency are very high. Conversely, if individuals have few rewarding social relationships that would be jeopardized by delinquent activity and anticipate no personal guilt or moral anxiety from such behavior, the costs are low. And because delinquent means are often more expedient means, low costs (i.e., weak controls) greatly increase the likelihood of delinquency.

The focus of control theories has thus been upon the socialization process, i.e., upon differences in the extent to which the norms have been internalized, providing weak or strong internal controls, and upon the degree of integration or bonding to conventional groups and activities that determines the strength of external controls on behavior. It is not the motivation for delinquency, but the strength of the internal and external controls that is problematic.

Although the focus of many early control theorists was upon the childhood socialization process and the internalization of conventional norms (internal controls), weak controls may result from other processes or conditions as well. Reiss identifies several conditions that result in weak controls and a vulnerability to delinquency:

> Delinquency results when there is a relative absence of internalized norms and rules governing behavior in conformity with the norms of the social system to which legal penalties are attached, a breakdown in previously established controls, and/or a relative absence of or conflict in social rules or techniques for enforcing such behavior in the social groups or institutions of which the person is a member [1951: 196].

In sum, weak controls may be a consequence of (1) the failure to develop internal controls during childhood; (2) the breakdown or weakening of previously established internal controls, particularly during adolescence; and/or (3) social disorganization in particular social units that results in weak external controls. In most instances, control theorists focus upon adolescent bonds to the family, school, community organizations, and future work roles as the major external sources of social control influencing youths' vulnerability to delinquency. Personal attitudes, values, and beliefs are the primary sources of internal control. At the individual level of explanation, the influence of formal agencies of social control (e.g., the police and courts) is mediated in part by personal beliefs such as respect for the law and attitudes toward the police, and in part by external controls in the form of perceived risks of police apprehension and severity of punishment by the justice system.

THE INTEGRATION OF STRAIN
AND CONTROL PERSPECTIVES

Kornhauser's (1978) review of the historical development and logical structure of sociological theories of delinquency led her to conclude that strain and control are both variants of social disorganization theory. Although acknowledging their differences, she notes that their logical structures do not preclude their integration.

> The strain and control variants of social disorganization theory are very different, but they do not begin from such opposed premises that their combination is precluded [Kornhauser, 1978: 46].

The primary difference between strain and control perspectives is that strain assumes a constant socialization outcome and variable strain whereas control theory assumes a variable socialization outcome and constant strain. Current strain models assume that all youths are adequately bonded to the family, school, and community, and are committed to conventional norms. The source of delinquency lies in youths' differential opportunities or successes in realizing these goals through conventional means. In contrast, control theory assumes a constant strain and variable levels of bonding to the family, school, and community, and a differential commitment to conventional norms.

In reviewing their logical structures, Kornhauser argues that the constant strain assumption is neither warranted nor necessary to control theory:

> The strain theorist rightly protests that the motivation to deviate is not in fact the same for everyone. It is, I think, plausible to assume that strain is a variable and it is not logically necessary for control theory to assume otherwise. The gratification-deprivation balance cannot really be identical for all. . . . Control

theory must, I think, grant that strain is a variable not a constant
[1978: 47-48].

Granting that strain is indeed variable, Kornhauser goes on to
argue that control theory is the more general perspective and
that it is not necessary to consider the variation in strain; i.e.,
that variations in controls are adequate to account for delinquency without reference to variations in strain. Because we
disagree with this conclusion, it is important to consider Kornhauser's argument in some detail.

Kornhauser presents two arguments for the position that
control theory can ignore variation in strain as a cause of delinquency. First, she argues that the variation in strain is relatively
limited compared to variation in controls, and therefore delinquency is primarily a function of social controls. Second, she
argues that strain causes delinquency by weakening controls,
i.e., that strain results in an attenuation of previously strong
controls, and that the weakening of such controls causes delinquency. Strain is thus one possible antecedent cause of weak
controls but adds no independent explanatory power to the
control explanation of delinquency. On the other hand, weak
controls affect delinquency independent of the presence or
absence of strain because strain is only one source of weak
controls. Control theory thus incorporates all the explanatory
power of strain theory without specific reference to strain.

Although we may question Kornhauser's first argument on
empirical grounds (as we will shortly), it is also unwarranted on
logical grounds. First, even if there were a more limited variation in strain, that fact does not logically preclude strain being
an independent causal factor in delinquency. The critical question for integration is whether strain accounts for any variation
in delinquency that is independent of social controls, not whether
strain or bonding is the more plausible or stronger causal influence. It is thus possible to argue that strain is a cause without
denying that weak controls are a stronger cause. Second, the
limited variation argument does not even support the position
that greater variation in bonding logically requires that it be a

stronger cause of delinquency. There may be more variation in the music preferences or level of sugar intake among adolescents than in their levels of family bonding, for example, but that fact does not insure or logically require that music preferences or sugar intake levels be more highly predictive of delinquency than family bonding. The amount of variation in an explanatory variable may have little significance for the strength of that variable's predictive relationship to other variables.

The second argument is more difficult to set aside. First we agree that strain theorists view strain as a source of attenuation on previously strong controls. Both Cloward and Ohlin, and Elliott and Voss make such claims (see Cloward and Ohlin, 1960: 108-109; Elliott and Voss, 1974: 28). We acknowledge, therefore, that the effect of strain is, at least in part, mediated by weak controls. But the critical question is whether the *entire* causal effect of strain works through an attenuation on controls. It is on this issue that we disagree with Kornhauser and argue for a synthesis of control and strain perspectives in the integrated model. The difference between the pure control model postulated by Kornhauser and an integrated control-strain model is depicted in Figure 2.1.

The integrated model does stipulate that strain leads to weak controls and that part of its effect on delinquency is an indirect effect mediated by weak controls. It differs from a pure control model, however, by specifying a direct causal path from strain to delinquency. The pure control model depicted here is based upon the sources of weak control proposed earlier by Reiss (1951) in which strain leads to an attenuation of existing controls but is only one possible antecedent cause of weak social control. Inadequate socialization and social disorganization are alternative causes. Further, social disorganization in the environment is postulated to be another cause of strain as suggested by Kornhauser (1978).

We believe the integrated control-strain model is defensible on both logical and empirical grounds. On logical grounds, if

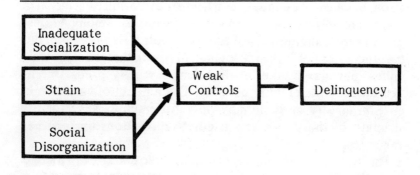

A. Pure Control Model

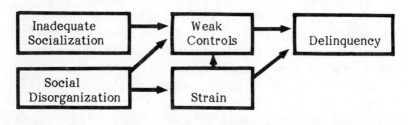

B. Integrated Control-Strain Model

Figure 2.1

one concedes (as Kornhauser does) that there is variation in both the motivation for delinquency (strain) and restraints on nonnormative behavior (social controls), the youths most vulnerable to delinquency should be those characterized by the combination of high motivation for delinquency and weak restraints on this behavior. The assertion that strain sometimes produces a weakening of controls is perfectly consistent with the model's claim that the joint occurrence of strain and weak controls generates a higher probability of delinquency than either alone. In this sense, strain as a source of attenuation on controls differs from other sources of weak controls because it simultaneously provides a motivation for delinquency. Inadequate socialization or social disorganization are alternative sources of weak control (Reiss, 1951); but these sources provide no direct or positive motivation for delinquency, and their influences are entirely mediated by strain and weak social controls.

In order to maintain logical consistency for a pure control model, one must argue that although there is variation in motivation for delinquency, its effect on delinquency is not independent of variation in restraints. This is essentially Kornhauser's argument when she claims that strain's effect on delinquency is totally mediated by weak controls.

EMPIRICAL SUPPORT FOR AN INTEGRATED CONTROL-STRAIN MODEL

Empirical support for the proposed synthesis of strain and control perspectives requires that strain must account for some variation in delinquency that is independent of that explained by variation in restraints. Although there are relatively few studies that have included both types of variables and undertaken the types of analyses necessary to address this question, those available do provide support for an integrated model as opposed to a pure control model.

First, we turn to Hirschi's analysis of the relationship between educational aspirations, educational expectations, and delinquency (self-reported and official). These data (see Table 2.1) are among the most frequently cited as evidence supporting a control model as opposed to a strain model (e.g., Kornhauser, 1978). They are particularly relevant to a comparison of the effects of strain and control because these two models postulate different relationships between aspirations and delinquency. For control theory, high aspirations represent a commitment to conventional goals and conventional lines of action—evidence of bonding that is postulated to reduce the probability of delinquency. Control theory thus predicts a simple inverse relationship between aspirations and delinquency. Strain theory, in contrast, posits a direct conditional relationship between

TABLE 2.1
Percentage Delinquent by Educational Aspirations and Expectations:
The Richmond Youth Study*

Educational Expectations		College Graduation	Some College	Less Than College	Total
College Graduation	SRD**	39(607)	--(6)	--(5)	38(618)
	Official	12(616)	--(6)	--(6)	12(628)
Some College	SRD	42(174)	44(196)	--(12)	42(382)
	Official	18(177)	18(200)	--(12)	17(389)
Less than College	SRD	58(29)	63(33)	56(151)	58(213)
	Official	13(29)	49(35)	33(159)	33(233)
Total	SRD	40(810)	46(235)	51(168)	43(1213)
	Official	13(822)	22(241)	29(177)	17(1240)

*Adapted from Table 60, p. 172, *The Causes of Delinquency* (Hirschi, 1969).
**SRD = one or more self-reported offenses, any offense; Official = one or more police contacts, any offense.

aspirations and delinquency: High aspirations in combination with low expectations generate strain and an increased likelihood of delinquency; high aspirations with high expectations or low aspirations (regardless of expectations) involve no strain and, hence, no motivation for delinquency. A test of these alternative explanations thus represents a crucial test; i.e., a direct comparison of competing hypotheses.

Hirschi (1969) claims that the data in Table 2.1 provide support for control theory but not for strain theory. First, he notes that the variation in strain is quite restricted, with only 19 percent of his sample perceiving any substantial discrepancy between educational aspirations and expectations. He then concludes:

Frustrated educational aspirations therefore cannot be an important antecedent of delinquency in the present sample ... there being insufficient variation on the independent variable to account for more than a small fraction of the variation in delinquency [1969: 172].

This argument is similar to that of Kornhauser discussed earlier. The fact that only 19 percent of the sample experienced strain whereas 43 percent were classified as delinquent may be used to argue that the variation in strain is insufficient to account for a major portion of the variation in delinquency, but it certainly does not permit one to conclude that strain is not a cause of delinquency. In fact, we question Hirschi's assertion that the observed variation in strain limits its explanatory power to "a small fraction" of the variation in delinquency. Indeed, the variation in aspirations is not as great as that for delinquency, with only 33 percent having aspirations for less than college graduation. If the delinquency classification results in 43 percent of the sample being defined as delinquent, then *neither* aspirations nor aspiration-opportunity discrepancies is likely to be a major cause of delinquency in this sample. On the other hand, when Hirschi uses an official classification of delinquents, the rate of delinquency is 17 percent, and *either* strain or control could logically account for all of the variance in this measure of delinquency. The "limited variation" argument is thus dependent upon the measure of delinquency used.

If the relationship between strain and delinquency in these data is weak, so is the relationship between aspirations and delinquency. Although the relationship between aspirations and self-reported delinquency in Table 2.1 is statistically significant, aspirations account for less than one percent of the variation in self-reported delinquency—hardly very compelling evidence or grounds for arguing for the superiority of a control as compared to a strain perspective.[1] Given the organization of the data in the table, the relationship between strain and self-reported delinquency is not significant; but if strain is defined as having some college aspirations but not expecting to go to college (i.e., collapsing the "some college" and "college" categories), the relationship is significant ($\chi^2 = 9.2$; Phi $= .09$, $p \leq .01$) and also accounts for about one percent of the variance in delinquency. Both strain and aspirations are significantly related to official delinquency, but again account for only a small proportion of the variation.

More relevant to the central issue at hand, these data demonstrate that variation in strain is related to variation in delinquency

among those with high aspirations. Among youths aspiring to
be college graduates, those experiencing strain have a substantially higher rate of delinquency than do those with no strain;
likewise, among those aspiring to some college, youths experiencing strain are substantially more likely to be delinquent.
Hirschi also cross-classified youth on the basis of fathers'
attained education and youths' expected educational attain-
ment. In this analysis he found that the two groups with the
highest rates of delinquency were the sons of college graduate
fathers who did not expect to graduate from college (1969:
173). There is a clear interaction between strain and aspirations
in both of these analyses.

A similar analysis with data from the longitudinal delinquency and dropout study by Elliott and Voss (1974) is presented
in Table 2.2. In this study, the delinquency classification based
upon self-reported offenses involves a serious prevalence
dichotomy rather than a general prevalence dichotomy as used
by Hirschi. This is because 90 percent of this sample of 2,617
junior high school students (males and females) reported one or
more delinquent acts on the self-report delinquency checklist.
This checklist included 19 items, whereas Hirschi's checklist
included only six items. This raises some questions about the
accuracy and theoretical relevance of a delinquent/nondelin-
quent classification when a small number of offense items is
used in the classification.[2] The use of a serious (felony) prevalence dichotomy in the Elliott-Voss study resulted in a delinquency rate that was very similar to that in the Hirschi study
(44 percent compared to 43 percent delinquent), although
Hirschi used a dichotomy based upon any self-reported delinquency. The second definition of delinquency is identical for
both studies—one or more official police contacts.

The data in Table 2.2 involve aspirations and expectations
for educational goals reported by the sample in the ninth grade
and self-reported and official delinquency over the next three
years (grades 10 to 12). The level of strain reported by these
youths is greater than that observed for boys in the Richmond
Youth Study, with nearly 30 percent perceiving some aspiration-expectation disjunction. Approximately 58 percent of

TABLE 2.2
Percentage Delinquent by Educational Aspirations and Expectations*

Educational Expectations		College Graduation	Some College	Less Than College	Total
College Graduation	SRD**	38(963)	41(17)	0(1)	38(981)
	Official	6(963)	0(17)	0(1)	6(981)
Some College	SRD	43(368)	40(409)	30(22)	42(799)
	Official	10(368)	6(409)	9(22)	8(799)
Less than College	SRD	57(156)	50(234)	54(392)	53(782)
	Official	10(156)	15(234)	7(392)	10(782)
Total	SRD	41(1487)	44(660)	53(415)	44(2562)
	Official	7(1487)	9(660)	7(415)	8(2562)

*Elliot and Voss, 1974.
**SRD = one or more serious (felony) self-reported offenses; official = one or more police contacts, any offense.

these youths aspire to graduate from college. The variation in strain is thus greater in this sample than in Hirschi's sample.

The relationship between aspirations and the self-reported delinquency classification in Table 2.2 is significant ($\chi^2 = 18.23$, 2DF, $p \leq .001$, $V = .08$), as is the relationship between strain and delinquency ($\chi^2 = 4.97$, 1DF, $p \leq .05$, Phi $= .04$). Official arrest rates are substantially lower in this study than in the Hirschi study (8 as compared to 17 percent). For this measure of delinquency, the relationship between aspirations and delinquency is not significant, whereas the relationship between strain and delinquency is significant ($\chi^2 = 21.63$, 1DF, $p \leq .001$, Phi $= .09$).

Except for the higher incidence of strain in this study and the failure to find a significant relationship between aspirations and police contact, the results are generally consistent with the earlier Hirschi analysis. There is again a clear interaction of strain and aspiration level on delinquency. Within each aspiration level in which strain is possible, youths experiencing strain are more likely to be delinquent than youths not experiencing strain. The relationship between strain and delinquency, holding aspiration level constant, is as strong or stronger than the general aspiration-delinquency relationship. Again, the highest rates of delinquency involve youths reporting aspiration-expectation discrepancies. In one case (official delinquency), the combination of moderate aspirations (some college) and strain produces the highest rate of delinquency; in the other (self-reported delinquency), it is the high aspirations-high strain combination that generates the highest rate of delinquency.

Hirschi presents a similar analysis of differences in delinquency rates by occupational aspirations and expectations (1969: 183). These data produce the same general results as described above; i.e., evidence of a strain-aspiration interaction within each aspiration category (in which differences in strain could exist). Those experiencing strain had higher mean self-reported frequencies than those not experiencing strain.

At only one point does Hirschi acknowledge the interaction between strain and bonding variables. In a separate analysis limited to boys expecting to go to college, Hirschi reports on an interaction between parental pressure and grades: Among those receiving good grades, the greater the parental pressure, the lower the delinquency; among those receiving poor grades, the greater the parental pressure, the greater the delinquency. The combination of high educational aspirations, high parental pressure for achievement, and poor school performance was associated with very high rates of delinquency; high aspirations, high parental expectations, and good grades were associated with low rates of delinquency. Hirschi then acknowledges, "and we have again uncovered a small group whose delinquency could be interpreted as resulting from a condition of strain" (1969: 177).

It is not surprising that Hirschi makes no reference to the obvious interaction in his educational and occupational aspiration-expectation data (for example, see Table 2.1). His focus was generally upon a comparison of strain, control, and cultural deviance models to determine which model received the most compelling and consistent support. We have only minor quarrels with his general conclusion that his data and analyses are more supportive of control than strain theory if they are viewed as competing explanations. However, Hirschi's data appear to be even more supportive of an integrated control-strain model. It appears that the combination of strain and weak controls could account for more variation in delinquency than either a pure strain or control model alone.

In sum, these crucial test data from Hirschi (1969) and Elliott and Voss (1974), although not definitive, do provide support for an integrated control-strain model: (1) the explanatory power of the control and strain variables was generally similar;[3] (2) there was obvious variation in strain within levels of bonding, and this variation was systematically related to variation in delinquency; and (3) the combination of strain and weak controls produced the highest probabilities of delinquency in three of the four analyses.[4] All of these findings are contrary to Kornhauser's argument and the claims of a pure control model.

There are a number of other studies that have examined the relationship between educational (and occupational) aspirations, expectations, and delinquency (e.g., Elliott, 1962; Clark and Wenninger, 1962; Reiss and Rhodes, 1963; Short, 1964; Spergel, 1964, 1967; Stinchcombe, 1964; Short et al., 1965; Wiatrowski, 1978). In general, the results of these studies are similar to those of Hirschi and Elliott and Voss reviewed above; high rates of delinquency were typically observed for both the low aspiration condition and the high aspiration with low expectation condition (see Liska, 1971). Thus, there is little support in this body of research findings for either a pure strain or a pure control model. The findings are, however, generally consistent with an integrated control-strain model.[5]

A problem with the previous analyses is that they involve a single measure of a causal variable and a single hypothesis from each theory. A more definitive test for an independent effect of strain requires a more general test in which multiple hypotheses and measures of causal variables are considered. There are several such analyses involving multiple regression and path analysis approaches to determine the independent effects of strain given a set of control variables.[6]

Cernkovich (1978) examined the predictive utility of pure strain and control models as well as an integrated model. The analysis was limited to four variables: A measure of SES, a scale of perceived blockage to conventional goals (strain), and two scales representing social control variables. The delinquency measure involved a 30-item self-reported delinquency checklist that was scored so as to take into account both the frequency and seriousness of offenses. Cernkovich completed a series of stepwise regression analyses in which the order of strain and control predictors was reversed. Based upon these analyses he concluded that strain and control as models each account for significant, though small, proportions of the variance in delinquency (strain accounts for 8 percent; control for 13 percent). Further, when control variables were entered into the stepwise analysis first, the addition of the strain variable produced a small but significant increase in explained variance.

This stepwise procedure provides a rather conservative test of the independent effects of strain because all shared variance was assigned to the control variables. But these data clearly support an integrated model: (1) there was a small but significant independent effect of strain on delinquency, and (2) the combined effect of strain and control variables accounted for more variance in delinquency than did either a pure strain or control model. Based upon these data, Cernkovich suggests an integrated model that is very similar to the one proposed here, in which strain causes delinquency both directly and through an attenuation of social controls.

In a partial replication of the Cernkovich study, Segrave and Hastad (1983) examined the independent and combined explanatory power of a set of strain and social control variables. The sample of this study involved 1802 high school students in an East coast city. Segrave and Hastad employed the same four predictor measures used by Cernkovich and a similar stepwise regression procedure in which the order of strain and control predictors was varied. In this analysis, strain predictors accounted for 6 to 7 percent of the explained variance in self-reported delinquency. Control predictors accounted for 12 to 13 percent of the explained variance. The combined set of predictors explained 15 percent of the variance. The explanatory power of strain predictors was thus 2 to 3 percent when controlling for social control predictors. The explanatory power of social control predictors was 7 to 8 percent when controlling for strain predictors. These results are very similar to those reported earlier by Cernkovich, and again provide empirical support for an integration of strain and control perspectives.

Eve (1978) used a slightly different approach to assess the combined predictive power of strain and social control variables in the explanation of delinquency. This study involved 300 eleventh- and twelfth-graders in a suburban high school. Two measures of deviance were used: A traditional deviance scale comprised of six offense items including such things as cheating on exams, skipping classes, and fighting; and a measure of drug use. Multiple measures of strain and social control were used. The strain measures included economic strain, educational strain, and strain relative to expected marital status and school grades. Twenty-three social control measures were designed to represent Hirschi's (1969) four dimensions of the social bond: Attachment, belief, commitment, and involvement. The three strongest strain variables were combined into a strain index, and the seven strongest control variables were combined into a control index. A six-item scale reflecting the degree of adherence to the youth subculture was also used in the analysis as an index of culture conflict.

Eve reports that all three of these indices were significantly related to both measures of deviance, with the control index being the strongest predictor. He then considered the hypothesis proposed by Kornhauser that the relationship between strain and delinquency was explained by the level of social control. He tested this hypothesis by controlling for the level of social control and recalculating the correlation (r) between strain and deviance. The results of this test indicated that partialing on level of control specified the relationship between the strain index and the deviance scale (r = .25, p $\leq$ .001); among those with strong controls the correlation was .11 (p $\leq$ .001); among those with weak controls, the correlation was .31 (p $\leq$ .001). The relationship between strain and deviance was thus substantially weaker, but still significant, among youth with strong controls. Among those with weak controls, the strain-deviance relationship was increased substantially relative to the general relationship.

These findings are clearly at odds with Kornhauser's position. Given her argument, we would expect both conditional relationships to be nonsignificant, indicating that the general strain-deviance relationship was explained or interpreted by differences in control (Hyman, 1955). The finding that partial-

ing on level of control specified the general relationship is
consistent with the expectations of the integrated model.

When drug use was the dependent variable, the conditional
relationships both declined. The general correlation between
strain and drug use was .21 (p ≤ .001); among those with strong
controls, this correlation was .02 (nonsignificant); among those
with weak controls it was .19 (p ≤ .03). These findings are
partially supportive of Kornhauser's position. Among those
with strong controls, variation in strain was unrelated to drug
use. However, variation in strain continued to be significantly
related to drug use among those with weak controls. With
regard to drug use, the results are thus mixed and only partially
supportive of an integrated model. Nevertheless, Eve concluded:

> It is apparent that all three theoretical perspectives account for
> some significant proportion of the variation in traditional high
> school deviance as well as drug use. Thus the attempt in recent
> years to prove one theory correct but the other two wrong may
> be nonproductive [1978: 9].

SUMMARY

There is little empirical support for Kornhauser's contention
that the effects of strain are entirely mediated by weak controls
and that strain has no unique or independent causal influence
on delinquency beyond that exerted by weak controls. On the
contrary, there is substantial evidence that strain has an independent causal effect on delinquency and, when combined with
control variables in an integrated model, results in increased
predictive utility.

It is also clear that part of the effect of strain is mediated by
weak controls as stipulated in the integrated model, i.e., that
there is both a direct and an indirect causal path from strain to
delinquency, the latter going through weak controls. We thus
conclude, on both logical and empirical grounds, that strain
and control models can be successfully integrated into a more
general model that has greater predictive efficiency than either
pure model alone.

At the same time, it must be acknowledged that the overall predictive efficiency of the integrated control-strain model is still relatively weak. Based upon the studies reviewed, the net increase in predictive efficiency appears to be only 2 to 3 percent. Although this represents a relative increase in explained variance of 16 to 23 percent over that achieved by a pure control model, there is still an obvious need for improvement.

In our earlier research we attempted to integrate strain and social learning perspectives and found that the inclusion of social learning variables added substantially to the predictive power of strain variables (Elliott and Voss, 1974). A number of others have tested mixed models that combined specific measures of social learning (or differential association) variables with measures of strain and/or social control variables (Meade and Marsden, 1981; Braukmann et al., 1980; Johnstone, 1981; Akers, 1977; Simons et al., 1980; Poole and Regoli, 1979; Linden, 1978; Ginsberg and Greenley, 1978; Akers and Cochran, 1983; Aultman and Welford, 1979; Patterson and Dishion, 1984; La Grange and White, 1983; Conger, 1976, 1980; Linden and Hackler, 1973; Johnson, 1979). In general, these studies have found increased levels of explained variance in delinquent behavior. Although few of these studies involved a genuine theoretical integration of the theories involved,[7] they do suggest that a model integrating social learning or differential association with strain and control perspectives might well account for more explained variance in delinquency and drug use than any one of these theories. In the next chapter we present a brief description of social learning theory, discuss the logical problems involved in integrating this perspective with strain and control perspectives, and review existing empirical evidence for a proposed theoretical integration of all three perspectives.

NOTES

1. Statistical significance is based upon a chi square test with $p \leq .05$. Variance explained is estimated by squaring the Phi Coefficient for dichotomized variables.

2. National prevalence estimates indicate that over 80 percent of American youths report one or more offenses when a comprehensive self-report measure is used (Gold and Reimer, 1975; Elliott et al., 1981).

3. In the Hirschi analyses the time ordering of delinquency and aspirations/ expectations variables is the reverse of that postulated theoretically; i.e., the self-reported delinquency measure reflects acts occurring in the year *prior* to the point at which aspirations and expectations were measured. The official measure reflects police records in the two years *preceding* and one year *after* the measure of aspirations and expectations. In the Elliott and Voss study, the measures of aspirations and expectations were obtained when the cohort was in the ninth grade, and the delinquency measures (self-report and official) reflect delinquent acts occurring in the tenth to twelfth grades. With one exception, the strength of the relationships examined was as strong or stronger in the Elliott-Voss study in which aspirations and strain were in the correct predictive position. The exception involves the aspiration-official delinquency relationship that was not significant in the Elliott-Voss study, but was significant in the Hirschi study. In all cases the relationships were weak, with phi or contingency values ranging from .04 to .15.

4. Hirschi's conclusion from his data is clearly at odds with that presented here. He states (1969: 185): "Discrepancies between the students' hopes and expectations are either unrelated to delinquency or are related in the direction opposite to that which these theories [strain] lead us to expect." Yet, the only analyses he presents involving direct measures of aspiration-expectation discrepancies are those discussed here, and there is no evidence here that those experiencing strain had lower rates of delinquency than did those with no strain, either in general or within aspiration categories. His conclusion thus seems unsupported by his data.

5. Kornhauser (1978: 174-175) cites studies by Gold (1963) and Fredericks and Molnar (1969) as providing negative evidence for the strain hypothesis. However, neither study provides a proper test of the hypothesis. The fact that matched samples (by race and class) of youths known and unknown to the police do not differ with respect to perceived strain does not logically preclude a finding that youths in the general population who experience strain have a higher risk of delinquency than do those experiencing no strain.

6. There are also a number of multivariate tests including strain and social control variables with variables from other social psychological theories. Our interest here is on tests limited to strain and control variables. We will consider combinations of strain, control, and differential association or social learning variables in Chapter 3.

7. In some of these studies the investigators have acknowledged the differences in theoretical assumptions, and a few have suggested ways to reconcile at least some of the important differences (e.g., Conger 1976, 1980; Johnson, 1979; La Grange and White, 1983). Hawkins and Weis (1980), and Glaser (1979) have provided a partial integration in their theoretical models as well, but neither have reported on an empirical test of their model. In most instances, however, little attention is given to integrating these explanations at a conceptual, theoretical level.

3

The Integration of Strain, Control, and Learning Theories

SOCIAL LEARNING THEORY

In contrast to pure strain and control perspectives, social learning theory assumes neither a constant motivation for crime nor a constant socialization outcome. There is thus no inherent tendency toward either conformity or deviance from this perspective. Both types of behavior are viewed as outcomes of variations in the socialization process that result in differential social reinforcements for conventional and deviant behavior. The initiation and maintenance of both conforming and deviant behavior depends upon anticipated rewards and punishments for the behavior, and the rewards and punishments associated with alternative behaviors. These expectations are based upon earlier observed outcomes of this behavior and the conditions associated with variation in outcomes (i.e., reinforcement contingencies—facilitators and inhibitors). The decision to engage in either conforming or deviant behavior is thus viewed as the result of a differential social reinforcement; i.e., the perception that the balance of rewards and punishments for a given act is more favorable than those for other alternative acts in that situation or context (Akers, 1977; Akers et al., 1979).

From this perspective, delinquency is the result of a direct socialization to deviance. Youths are not pushed into delinquency by strain or are unable to resist a natural impulse toward delinquency because of weak social controls; rather, they observe and learn in group interactions that some delinquent behaviors are encouraged and rewarded by the group, and that the anticipated rewards outweigh the potential costs or punishments associated with these behaviors in particular situations or settings.

Although most social groups have a conventional orientation and provide social reinforcements for conforming behavior, others have an orientation that reinforces delinquent behavior (hereafter referred to as delinquent groups).[1] These latter groups provide a setting in which attitudes, motives, and rationalizations that tolerate or encourage delinquency are learned; delinquent behaviors are modeled; those circumstances that facilitate or inhibit a successful delinquent performance are identified; and social rewards and reinforcements are provided for these acts (Sutherland, 1947; Akers, 1977; Burgess and Akers, 1966; Conger, 1976; Bandura, 1969; Bandura and Walters, 1963; Rotter, 1954).

Most social learning theorists acknowledge that there are both social and nonsocial rewards and punishments. Yet the primary focus of most theoretical statements is upon social interactions or exchanges in which the real or anticipated actions and responses of other persons or groups provide the reinforcement for behavior. For the most part, nonsocial experiences of the individual are given meaning by these social exchanges; i.e., individuals come to perceive their experiences as rewards or punishments in light of the group's reactions or responses to them. Nonsocial experiences are thus mediated by social exchanges within the group.

Those individuals and groups that control the major sources of rewards and punishments during childhood and adolescence (i.e., the family, the school, and the peer group) are postulated to have the greatest influence upon adolescent behavior (Sutherland, 1947; Akers, 1977; Akers et al., 1979). It is the behavioral and normative orientations of these groups and the types of differential social reinforcements learned in each of these settings that are critical for the generation of delinquent or conforming behavior during adolescence. For the most part, neither the family nor the school is seen as a deviant learning context, i.e., as providing a direct socialization to delinquency;

with few exceptions, both are quite conventional in their normative orientations and types of behavior modeled and reinforced (Kornhauser, 1978; Zigler and Child, 1969; Kohn, 1959; Eve, 1975; Hirschi, 1969, Lerman, 1968).[2] The primary deviant learning context is the adolescent peer group; the greatest variation in normative orientations, delinquent behavior patterns, and social reinforcements for delinquent behavior are found in this social context.

This is not to say that the individual's experiences in the family and school are always supportive of conventional behavior. Individuals' experiences in these conventional contexts may, in fact, provide little positive reinforcement for conventional behavior and may provide reinforcement for deviant behaviors even if there is no direct modeling of these behaviors by these socializing agents (e.g., failure at school may support cheating on exams even though this is not modeled or approved of by teachers). Likewise, exposure to delinquent groups may result in a set of negative anticipated consequences from delinquent acts. Thus, learning theory does not postulate a uniform, all-powerful socializing impact of the group on the individual. But without some exposure to delinquent behavior patterns and some social reinforcements for these behaviors, delinquent acts are unlikely to be initiated and even less likely to be maintained over time. Both conforming and deviant behavior patterns are maintained by social reinforcements.

In sum, learning theory postulates that there is a direct socialization to delinquency primarily within adolescent peer groups. Although there are obvious variations in socialization experiences in other contexts, it is primarily the variation in exposure to delinquent behavior patterns in the peer group that results in (1) differences in the range and balance of delinquent and conforming behaviors in the individual's behavioral repertoire; (2) differences in the reinforcement expectations for delinquent and conventional forms of behavior; and (3) differences in the perception of the contingencies associated with these reinforcements. Individual patterns of delinquent behavior are thus initiated and maintained by social reinforcements for these behaviors provided by individuals and groups in the larger society.

THE INTEGRATION OF STRAIN, CONTROL, AND LEARNING THEORIES

The historical tradition of social learning theory is clearly different from that of strain and control theories (Kornhauser, 1978; Akers, 1977; Conger, 1980). Yet there are some similarities in the basic assumptions of control and learning theories. First, both view delinquency as the result of variations in socialization experiences. Both theories assert that the most important source of controls or reinforcements are found in the web of social relationships. Second, both view behavior as resulting from a rational evaluation of the relative costs and rewards associated with particular acts. Thus both theories employ some version of differential costs and reinforcements resulting from variations in socialization as an explanation for behavior. The mechanism that maintains conforming behavior is the same for both—a higher differential reinforcement for conforming as compared to deviant acts. Conger (1980) thus notes that the delinquency prevention strategies suggested by control and learning theories are identical: Both involve strengthening social bonds to conventional groups and activities so as to increase social rewards for conforming behavior and costs (punishment) for delinquent behavior.

Although the explanations for conforming behavior are similar, there are clear differences in the explanations for deviant behavior. Control theory assumes a natural motivation to deviance; delinquency occurs because of weak or nonexisting bonds to conventional norms and groups, and the resulting *absence* of conventional restraints on behavior. The only recognized source of bonding or control involves conventional socializing groups and institutions; the only recognized sources of social reinforcements for behavior are conventional social groups and institutions.

In contrast, learning theory postulates the presence of both conventional and deviant socializing agents, both conventional and deviant learning environments, and bonding to both conventional and deviant groups. The same basic socialization processes operate in both learning contexts. The individual may become socially bonded (i.e., involved and committed) to conforming or deviant groups, and as a result may receive social reinforcements for either conventional or deviant behavior (or both); they may also come to anticipate negative consequences for either conventional or deviant acts. There is no need to assume an inherent or natural predisposition to deviance because deviance is learned and maintained in the same way that conforming behavior is learned and maintained.

Although both learning and control theories view delinquency as a result of variations in socialization, the specific source of variation is thus different. For control theory the content of socialization is uniformly conventional and the variation is in how well the socialization process works; socialization is "always more or less effective, never perfect" (Kornhauser, 1978: 39). Thus youths vary in their ability to learn, internalize norms, and maintain the personal relationships required for social integration (social disability argument); parents vary in their ability or skill for adequately socializing their children (defective socialization argument); and there are variations in social conditions and circumstances, some of which are more favorable to learning, internalization, and social integration than others (the social disorganization argument).

For learning theory, it is variation in the *content* of socialization that accounts for delinquency; it is variation in exposure to delinquent and conforming groups and variations in *what* is learned, internalized, and socially reinforced that is critical for the explanation of delinquency. Although learning theorists do not deny variation in the effectiveness of socialization, they do not consider this source of variation to be the major cause of delinquency because it may characterize the socialization process in either conventional or deviant contexts.[3]

The resolution of this difference is critical to an integration of control and learning theories. Is delinquency the result of a defective socialization in conventional groups that results in weak restraints on an inherent predisposition to delinquency; or are delinquents adequately socialized youths who have been exposed to delinquent as well as conventional behavior patterns, who have developed stronger bonds to delinquent than conventional persons and groups, and who have learned that under some circumstances the anticipated social rewards for delinquent behavior outweigh the anticipated costs?

Our integrated model takes the latter perspective; i.e., that delinquency is the result of a differential bonding to conventional and delinquent groups. Such a position requires a modification in the pure form of control theory so as to take into account the normative orientation of the group to which one is bonded; i.e., youth may be strongly bonded to conventional groups with little or no modeling of delinquency and uniformly negative responses to this type of behavior, or they may be more strongly bonded to groups in which delinquent behavior is frequently modeled and positively rewarded.

Given our earlier position that the family is a conventional learning context and the adolescent peer group is the primary setting in which one is exposed to pro-delinquent influences, there is a logical time ordering in the experiences of youth in these two social contexts. One's bonding relationship to conventional groups, particularly the family, is thus largely determined prior to one's exposure to delinquent influences in the peer group, and the strength of these bonds may well be a causal factor in the selection of companions or the recruitment of the individual by deviant groups. Given this life stage sequence, we propose that bonding to delinquent or conventional peers is conditioned by the strength of one's prior bonding to conventional norms and groups, particularly the family and the school. At the same time, the integrated model asserts that weak conventional bonding by itself is insufficient to cause a sustained involvement in delinquent behavior and that it is the joint occurrence of weak bonding to conventional groups/norms and strong bonding to deviant persons and groups that maximizes the probability of a sustained involvement in delinquent behavior. Only under this set of circumstances is the individual both free from conventional restraints and positively rewarded for delinquent acts.

LOGICAL SUPPORT FOR
THE INTEGRATION

There are logical and empirical grounds for the proposed modification of control theory. First, control theory's assumption of a constant motivation for deviance is an unreasonable assumption. We noted earlier in our discussion of integrating strain and control theories that Kornhauser (1978: 47) acknowledges that it is more reasonable to assume that the motivation for delinquency is not the same for everyone. Further, the empirical evidence presented earlier provided no empirical support for a constant motivation assumption. Finally, Hirschi's (1969) test of control theory led him to this same conclusion:

> The theory underestimated the importance of delinquent friends; it overestimated the significance of involvement in conventional activities. Both of these miscalculations appear to stem from the same source, the assumption of "natural motivation" to delinquency. If such natural motivation could legitimately be assumed, delinquent friends would be unnecessary and involvement in conventional activities would curtail the commission of delinquent acts. In other words, failure to incorporate some notions of what delinquency does *for* the adolescent probably accounts for the failure of the theory in these areas [1969: 230, emphasis in original].

Clearly then, the natural motivation assumption is untenable, and control theory must be modified to account for variation in motivation for delinquency. The acknowledgement that youths may become bonded to groups in which delinquent behavior is socially rewarded provides an explanation of what delinquency does *for* youth. Just as bonding to conventional groups provides positive rewards for law-abiding behavior, bonding to delinquent groups provides positive rewards for delinquent behavior.

Second, a long-standing logical criticism of pure control theory has been that an absence of restraints on behavior, by itself, cannot account for the specific form or content of any resulting behavioral adaptation (Cohen and Short, 1966). Why do some youths with weak conventional bonds turn to crime or drug use, others to various types of unconventional but legal behavior, and still others maintain an essentially conforming pattern of behavior? The natural motivation assumption fails to account for the variations in behavior among those with weak bonds to conventional society. The argument that delinquents have become more strongly bonded to delinquent than conventional groups does provide an explanation for this variation. Not all youths with weak bonds to conventional groups are expected to adopt a pattern of behavior that includes delinquent acts; only those who subsequently become bonded to groups that provide reinforcements for these acts are predicted to adopt a delinquent behavior pattern.

If control theory is modified to acknowledge variation in the content of socialization in addition to variation in the effectiveness of socialization, the relationship of each type of variation to delinquency must be explicated. Figure 3.1 indicates the expected outcomes for the combined effects of these two sources of variation in simplified form. As noted in Figure 3.1, the effectiveness of socialization varies in both conventional and delinquent learning contexts. Those factors identified by control theory as contributing to ineffective socialization should operate equally in both contexts. Frustrated personal needs or goals, unskilled or inadequate socializing agents, social disabilities in particular youths, and social disorganization in the learning context (e.g., unstable membership, weak leadership structure, strong environmental stress, etc.) should all contribute to low bonding, whether the socialization context is conventional or deviant.

Figure 3.1 indicates that the youth most likely to engage in delinquent behavior are those with weak bonds to conventional groups and strong bonds to groups with a delinquent orienta-

Conventional Socialization
Outcome

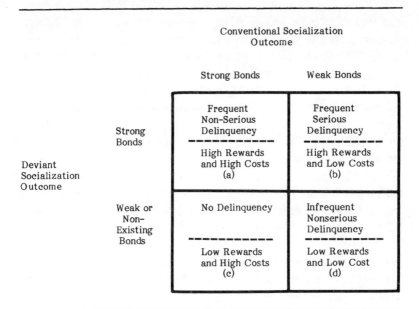

Figure 3.1: Expected Delinquency Outcomes by Variation in the Content and Effectiveness of Socialization

tion (Cell b). Likewise, those least likely to engage in delinquent behavior are those with strong bonds to conventional groups and weak or nonexisting bonds to groups with a delinquent orientation (Cell c). In the first case, delinquent behaviors (as well as conventional acts) are rewarded by the group, and there are few conventional restraints on this type of behavior; in the second case, the behavioral set that is rewarded is not likely to include any delinquent acts, and the cost associated with these acts is high. However, both types of youth are integrated into a web of social relationships and are receiving social reinforcements for their behavior.

Those characterized by weak bonds to both conventional and delinquent groups (Cell d) have little positive reinforcement for *either* delinquent or conventional behavior and few conventional restraints on delinquency. Such youths are marginal to all social groups and institutions. Although they may not be receiving many reinforcements for conventional behavior, neither are they receiving reinforcements for delinquent behavior. There may be some occasional exploratory involvement in nonserious forms of delinquent behavior because the social costs for such behavior is low; but there is no informal or formal group mechanism to maintain any sustained involvement in such behavior, particularly with regard to the more serious forms of delinquency that are more likely to result in punitive sanctions from the police and court. In the absence of informal constraints or rewards from primary group relationships (which are the most powerful determinants of behavior), more formal control mechanisms present in the community (i.e., the police, school officials, and courts) remain and should serve to constrain the more serious forms of delinquent behavior. There are no social rewards to offset the potential costs of delinquency for isolated (weakly bonded) youth, and if nonsocial rewards are in fact mediated by social exchanges, there are no substantial benefits that can be derived from delinquent acts. We do expect some occasional minor violations from weakly bonded youth because the potential risks and costs are very low, but no serious delinquent acts are expected, nor is any sustained pattern of involvement in nonserious acts.

Finally, the integrated model postulates a type of youth who has strong bonds to both conventional and deviant others (Cell a). Control, strain, and learning theories are all rational theories; i.e., they all assume a rational view of man. Because our view of bonding includes the internalization of group norms and beliefs as well as involvement and commitment to these groups, strong bonding to both conventional and deviant groups over an extended period of time necessarily involves a dissonant state. It is possible that youths maintain this pattern of strong bonds to both conventional and deviant groups by a psychological and social compartmentalization of their lives; e.g., they are different persons when they are with parents or friends. However, we believe that this pattern of bonding is more typically a temporary state and often reflects a period in which commitments are changing. It may not be uncommon to be in this state for one or two years during adolescence but it is unlikely that individuals would remain in this state for a longer period, particularly as they move into the adult years. Youths characterized by this dissonant pattern of bonding have a double repertoire of values and norms that can be turned on and off depending on the social context. We would expect some limited delinquent activity for youth with this pattern of bonding. It should involve relatively nonserious, group-related types of delinquency that would demonstrate peer group affiliation and loyalty, but would not seriously jeopardize family or school relationships. There are some reinforcements for delinquency for these youth, but the costs associated with the serious forms of crime are also high.

EMPIRICAL SUPPORT FOR THE INTEGRATION: DIRECT SOCIALIZATION TO DELINQUENCY

Moral beliefs. The integration of control and learning theories that acknowledges variation in both the strength and normative orientation of bonding raises a number of empirical questions. First, is there any evidence for the direct socialization position; are there groups that provide positive reinforcements for delinquent acts?

This question should not be confused with the question about the reality of delinquent subcultures. A social learning model, although similar in some respects to a cultural deviance model (i.e., both posit a direct socialization to deviance), is not dependent upon the presence of a delinquent subculture, i.e., a subculture that endorses values in direct opposition to those endorsed by conventional society, in which delinquent acts are viewed as morally superior to conforming acts and prescribed by the subcultural values. There is little research evidence that delinquent youths see their delinquent behavior as morally superior to conventional behavior or that they personally espouse values that are truly oppositional to those of conventional society (Short and Strodtbeck, 1965; Hirschi, 1969; Kornhauser, 1978; Michael, 1963; Conklin, 1971; Rossi et al., 1974; Empey and Lubeck, 1968; Buffalo and Rogers, 1971; Gold, 1970; Lerman, 1968; Jensen and Rojek, 1980). But research does document the presence of delinquent youths and peer groups in which delinquent attitudes, skills, and behaviors are encouraged, rewarded, and modeled.

Although there is little evidence that delinquent groups directly challenge the ultimate "rightness" or moral superiority of conventional values and behavior, socialization processes in such groups do undermine the significance and salience of moral evaluations as determinants of behavior. This is accomplished in several ways. First, there is evidence that delinquent groups view the moral dimension of evaluation as irrelevant or inapplicable to their circumstances. Suttles found that moral evaluations are considered irrelevant to slum life:

> The subculture of the slum does not consist of moral evaluations that overturn the cannons of conventional morality. Slum subculture lacks an evaluative dimension and consists instead of cognitive orientations sought in a quest for order when the precepts of conventional morality are inapplicable [Suttles, 1968, as cited by Kornhauser, 1978: 224].

Suttles notes that gang boys in slum areas do not view criminal acts as "desirable" but rather as inevitable, a routinely occurring fact of life. If asked whether these criminal acts were "right" or "wrong" these youth would probably report that they were "wrong," but such an evaluation would have little relevance for their involvement in such behavior. The Schwendingers (1967) also report that when delinquent youths were asked to argue against the commission of an assault or robbery, they employed tactical (e.g., "will get caught") rather than moral arguments. Nondelinquent youth were much more likely to use moral arguments as reasons for not committing crimes. Buffalo and Rogers's (1971) study of inmates in training school also suggests that moral evaluations of behavior may be irrelevant for delinquent youth. These youths were presented with a series of hypothetical situations and asked (1) what they *should* do and then (2) what they *would* do. Their responses to the first question for the most part reflected conventional moral evaluations, yet their responses to the second question often involved delinquent acts. These youths were aware of the conventional moral evaluations, but such evaluations did not appear to be a major determinant of their anticipated behavior.

Second, there is some evidence that delinquent youth neutralize moral evaluations of their behavior on the grounds that their situation or circumstances excuse or justify this type of act (Matza, 1964; Ball, 1966; Hirschi, 1969; Hindelang, 1973; Minor, 1981). In the only predictive test of the relationship between neutralizing beliefs (excuse acceptance) and subsequent delinquent behavior, Minor (1981) found that those youth accepting excuses for delinquent behavior were more likely to engage in subsequent delinquent acts. This relationship was strongest among youth who expressed moral disapproval of the delinquent act in question. However, it was also found for those who did not disapprove and who had engaged in that behavior previously. Minor concludes that acceptance of excuses for delinquent acts changes one's moral evaluations of delinquent acts over time; i.e., those accepting these excuses for delinquency subsequently become less disapproving of these acts. The fact that excuse acceptance was related to subsequent delinquency for those who did not disapprove of these acts led Minor to suggest "that neutralizing excuse may not only *allow* deviance, but also *encourage* it" (1981: 313). We suggest that excuse acceptance is a part of the socialization experience in delinquent groups and serves to encourage delinquent behavior as an expected and approved outcome under certain conditions.

Third, there is evidence of a hierarchy of values among delinquent youths in which both conventional and delinquent abilities and behaviors are positively valued. The fact that virtually all adolescent groups, when asked to evaluate conforming and deviant acts, acknowledge the moral superiority of conforming behavior does not necessarily imply that delinquent acts are not valued or are negatively valued. A number of studies indicate that delinquent skills and behaviors are positively valued by delinquent groups (Short and Strodtbeck, 1965; Lerman, 1968; Wilson et al., 1965; Hindelang, 1970,

1974; Austin, 1977; Kornhauser, 1978; Minor, 1981). For example, Lerman (1968) asked youths from a New York slum area to choose the ability they most admired (now and 2 to 3 years ago) from a list that included both conventional (e.g., to get good grades; to do well in the job world) and deviant abilities (e.g., to make a fast buck; to make connections with a racket). Although getting good grades had the highest overall ranking among these youths at both times, 15 percent chose a deviant ability for the present and 26 percent chose a deviant ability for the earlier period. Further, admiring a deviant ability was related to a youth's involvement in delinquency. More relevant to the issue of positive reinforcement for delinquent acts, respondents were also asked how much their friends admired these abilities. A majority of these youths perceived that five or six deviant abilities (the exception being making connections with a racket) were attractive to their friends. Boys who perceived that their friends admired deviant abilities were more likely to have been involved in delinquent behavior than were those who preceived little admiration for these abilities by their friends. Although receiving good grades had the highest overall ranking for youths in this study, there was a subset of youths who valued a deviant ability most highly, and more importantly, most youths perceived that their friends valued deviant abilities. The perception that their friends value "making a fast buck," "being hard and tough," "finding kicks," and "outsmarting others" suggests a perceived social approval and reward for a number of delinquent acts (e.g., petty theft, simple assault, alcohol and drug use, con games, etc.).

Short and Strodtbeck (1965) also found that gang and non-gang boys evaluated conventional images (e.g., works for good grades and saves his money) equally highly. Although both groups evaluated conventional images higher than deviant images, gang boys rated the deviant images (e.g., makes easy money off pimping and uses drugs) higher than did the nongang boys. In sum, it appears that the hierarchy of values is different for delinquent and nondelinquent groups. Both groups evaluate conventional goals and skills similarly. They differ on their evaulations of unconventional goals and skills with delinquent groups placing more value on these goals and skills than non-delinquent groups. It appears that delinquent persons and groups endorse both conventional and unconventional values whereas nondelinquent persons and groups endorse only conventional values.

Although subcultural theories place a great emphasis upon the moral dimensions of beliefs, neither social learning nor control theories view this dimension of bonding as the only, or even a major, determinant of behavior (Jensen and Rojek, 1980; Linden and Hackler, 1973; Akers, 1977; Langer, 1976). Even if moral evaluations were relevant to behavior in delinquent groups, we would not expect this particular aspect of the belief bond to mediate all bonding influences on behavior. In fact the available evidence suggests that compared to the other dimensions of bonding, the belief dimension of bonding is seldom the strongest predictor of behavior (Hirschi, 1969; Krohn and Massey, 1980; Johnson, 1979; Johnstone, 1981; Empey, 1978; Thomas and Hyman, 1978; Meade and Marsden, 1981). Also, from a learning perspective the knowledge that one's behavior will be evaluated by others as "good" or "right" is only one of a number of possible social rewards and reinforcements for behavior. Conger thus notes:

> A social learning view is not antithetical to the notion that such beliefs [moral norms] should decrease the chance of juvenile deviance, but they certainly would be considered secondary to attachment and commitment in their influence [1980: 133].

Clearly, involvement, attachment, and commitment to conventional or delinquent groups have relevance for delinquency irrespective of what an adolescent personally believes or acknowledges to be right or wrong. Herein lies a critical difference between cultural deviance theories and social learning/bonding theories. One thing is clear: Many adolescents report involvement in delinquent acts even when they acknowledge that such acts are morally wrong (Jensen, 1972; Hindelang, 1974; Minor, 1981; Jessor and Jessor, 1977; Buffalo and Rogers, 1971; Jensen and Rojek, 1980). Socialization by delinquent persons and groups appears to attenuate the influence of personal moral evaluations on behavior but not reverse them (Jensen and Brownfield, 1983). A number of studies indicate that peer influence may override moral beliefs and have a stronger influence on behavior (Wheeler, 1967; Briar and Piliavin, 1965; Luckenbill and Sanders, 1977; Liska, 1974). In any case, the explanation for delinquent behavior appears to depend more heavily upon other dimensions of belief, group processes, and types of social reinforcements.

Other dimensions of belief. Although delinquent acts are not perceived as normative in a moral sense, delinquent youths do perceive that such behavior is normative in a statistical sense; i.e., they believe that most youth are involved in criminal acts. Although crime may not be viewed as moral behavior, it is nonetheless expected behavior. Gold (1970) asked a normal sample of youths to estimate the percentage of their friends and all youths who commit specific delinquent acts. Gold notes that nearly all respondents attributed more delinquency to their peers than they actually committed. He also found that the more delinquent a respondent, the greater the overestimate of delinquency among youth in general. For those involved in delinquent behavior, delinquent acts were perceived to be very frequent among all adolescents. In fact, delinquent youths typically saw themselves and their friends as less delinquent than teenagers in general. Gold suggests that delinquent youths justify their delinquent acts by perceiving that they are not much different from other teenagers in this regard. He goes on to note that this distorted perception may result from the fact that their friends are in fact more delinquent, and they assume that their friends' behavior is typical of other adolescents. Buffalo and Rogers (1971) report a similar finding, noting that delinquents in their sample perceived that "most boys their age" were involved in more delinquency than they were; and Lerman (1968) found that all boys in his sample believed that their friends admired delinquent abilities and skills. For those involved with delinquent groups, there may be a general sense of approval for these behaviors that results from the belief that everyone is involved in such behavior. Delinquency is thus viewed as normative behavior in the sense that it is seen as common to all youth and thus expected in a probabilistic sense. This type of normative expectation provides some justification for delinquent acts as one can hardly be singled out and condemned for doing what everyone is doing.

Modeling delinquent acts. The evidence that delinquent youths are exposed to more modeling of delinquency by their friends than are nondelinquent youths is substantial (Hirschi, 1969; Hardt and Peterson, 1968; Elliott, 1961; Gold, 1970; Hindelang, 1973; Elliott and Voss, 1974; Johnson, 1979, Glueck and Glueck, 1950; Erickson and Empey, 1965; Voss, 1964; Short, 1957; Krohn, 1974; Kandel, 1973; Kandel et al., 1978; Jessor, 1981; Jessor and Jessor, 1977; Knowles, 1979; Andrews and Kandel, 1979; Jensen, 1972; Jensen and Rojek, 1980; Johnstone, 1981; Akers et al., 1979). Reiss and Rhodes (1964), Conger (1976), and Akers et al. (1979) report even more direct evidence of modeling. Using sociometric groups (triads), Reiss and Rhodes found that the probability of an individual committing a specific kind of delinquent act depended upon the commission of that act by other group members.[4] Conger found that delinquent friends were more likely to engage in similar than dissimilar kinds of criminal acts, and Akers et al. found that the more respondents had observed parents, friends, and other "admired" models using alcohol or drugs, the more likely the respondent was to report using these substances.

Social approval for delinquent acts. Many of the above referenced studies indicate that delinquents also perceive social approval for delinquent acts from their friends. Hindelang (1970, 1974) found that youths engaging in each of a variety of delinquent acts were substantially more approving of these acts than were youths not engaging in them and that both types of youths perceived that their friends were equally or more approving of delinquent acts than they were themselves.[5] Analyzing data from a national sample of adolescents, Jessor

(1981) found a strong relationship between friends modeling a behavior and approving of that behavior, and the respondents reporting some involvement in that act. These two variables accounted for nearly all the explained variance in marijuana use, drunkenness, and a global measure of deviant behavior that included both serious and nonserious criminal acts. In an earlier longitudinal study, Jessor and Jessor (1977) report a similar finding. Buehler et al. (1966) and Akers et al. (1979) also present evidence that delinquents directly reinforce one another's delinquent behavior. In the Akers et al. study the perception of approving or disapproving attitudes on the part of parents and peers toward alcohol and marijuana use, together with anticipated rewards or punishments for these acts from parents and peers, accounted for 50 percent of the variance in alcohol use and 65 percent of the variance in marijuana use. Johnson's (1979) study also indicated that delinquents perceived social approval for delinquent acts from their friends. Johnson attempted to separate the influence of perceived approval for delinquency by friends from simply associating with delinquent friends. Based upon a factor analysis, he reports that friends' approval for delinquency and number of delinquent friends were not empirically discriminable; i.e., to have delinquents as friends is to perceive positive social rewards for delinquent behavior.

These data would appear to confirm the presence of persons and groups that provide positive reinforcements for delinquent behavior.[6] That such persons or groups provide rewards and support for delinquency is clearly contrary to the logic of a pure control model of delinquency, but consistent with an integrated control-social learning model that considers the conforming or delinquent orientation of persons and groups to which adolescents are bonded.

The strength of bonds to delinquent friends. The second empirical question raised by the integration of control and learning perspectives concerns the extent to which delinquent youths are truly bonded to other adolescents, whether they be delinquent or nondelinquent. A pure control model asserts that delinquent youths are unbonded youths, either unwilling to or incapable of developing and maintaining ties to other persons or groups and hence not subject to normal group influences and socialization processes (Hirschi, 1969; Kornhauser, 1978; Hansell and Wiatrowski, 1981). The integrated model asserts that delinquents are youths who have weak bonds to conventional persons and groups but strong bonds to deviant persons and groups. Both models view bonding to conventional groups as a deterrent to delinquency. At issue is the question of whether delinquent youths are strongly or weakly bonded to delinquent persons and groups.

Evidence for the pure control position is claimed by Hirschi (1969). Hirschi found that those who identified most closely with their friends were less likely to have committed delinquent acts. However, this relationship was very weak (Phi = .07) and does not control for the delinquent or nondelinquent orientation of friends.[7] In a second analysis, Hirschi looked at the number of self-reported delinquent acts by the number of delinquent friends and level of identification with friends. For those with three or more delinquent friends, there was again a weak negative relationship between level of identification (i.e., bonding) and self-reported delinquent acts. Hirschi concludes that these data confirm the control model assertion that delinquent youths are weakly bonded to delinquent peers.

In fact Hirschi's data provide little support for the pure control model. First, the negative relationship between identification with friends and delinquency held only for those with three or more delinquent friends; it did not hold for those with one or two delinquent friends. Second, an examination of the table reveals that the major determinant of self-reported delinquency was the variation in the number of friends who were delinquent; variation in identification had relatively little influence on self-reported delinquency. Third, in a reanalysis of the data in this table, Conger (1980) found that 83 percent of those subjects with one or more delinquent friends and 90 percent of those with no delinquent friends wanted to be like their best friend in at least some ways. The fact is that the vast majority of those with delinquent friends *did* identify with these friends. There is little evidence here that suggests a differential level of bonding to delinquent and nondelinquent friends. It is also the case that these data involve a single dimension of bonding. A general conclusion about differential bonding to delinquent and nondelinquent others certainly requires a more comprehensive set of bonding measures that reflect all of the theoretical dimensions of bonding.

A number of studies have found evidence consistent with the integrated model's position on bonding to delinquent peers. Linden (1978), using the same data set as Hirschi, reports on a number of different items reflecting peer relationships in an analysis of self-reported delinquency and social class. Two of these items assess how other students view the respondents' friends, and four of them reflect the respondents' ties to their friends. Our interest is primarily in the latter measures of peer bonding. For two of the measures (number of best friends and perceived loyalty of best friends) there was no relationship with self-reported delinquency. The third measure was similar to that used by Hirschi, reflecting whether or not respondents wanted to be like their best friends, and this measure of peer bonding was negatively correlated with self-reported delinquency. This finding thus confirms that reported earlier by Hirschi (1969). The final measure, time spent talking with friends, produced the strongest relationship with self-reported delinquency. Those who spent more time talking with friends tended to report higher levels of delinquency. Although delinquent boys may be less likely to idealize their friends than nondelinquent boys, they have similar numbers of best friends, perceive these friends to be equally loyal to them, and spend more time with them than do nondelinquent boys. Although there appear to be some differences in the nature of the bonds, it would clearly be misleading to conclude from these data that delinquent youths are weakly bonded to peers as compared to nondelinquent youth.

In a further analysis of the same body of data used by Hirschi, Jensen and Erickson (1978) found no association between peer commitment and delinquency among blacks; i.e., delinquents and nondelinquents had comparable levels of peer commitment. Conger (1976) also found no relationship between attachment to peers and delinquency. Krohn and Massey (1980) found no relationship between attachment to peers and nonserious delinquency, but a weak negative relationship ($r = -.10$) with a serious delinquency measure. Jessor and Jessor (1977) found no relationship between their measure of perceived support from friends and delinquency. Delinquent and nondelinquent youths were equally likely to perceive that their friends would be available when they needed help and encouragement and that their friends were interested in them. Figueira-McDonough et al. (1981) report a positive relationship between involvement in peer activities and delinquent behavior for both males and females. Further, Hindelang (1973), West and Farrington (1977), Elliott and Voss (1974), Empey and Lubeck (1971), Erickson and Empey (1965), and Rothstein (1962) all report a positive relationship between commitment to friends and delinquent behavior. These last studies suggest that delinquent youths may be *more* involved with and committed to their friends than are nondelinquent youth.

Jensen and Rojek (1980) point out that the measures of commitment or attachment used by Elliott and Voss (1974), Erickson and Empey (1965), and Empey and Lubeck (1971) all include some element of conflict (e.g., would you go along with your friends if they were getting you into trouble or breaking the law?), whereas the measure used by Hirschi (1969) and Krohn and Massey (1980) does not. They suggest that such measures include an attitude toward the proposed activity as well as the strength of commitment to the group, and this accounts for the positive relationship between such measures and delinquency. Jensen and Rojek cite a study by Jensen and Erickson (1978) to support this argument. Jensen and Erickson asked subjects whether they would go along with their friends or join their families if their families were planning on going to a show. There was no relationship between responses to this question and delinquency (although slightly more of those choosing "friends" reported delinquent acts). When subjects were asked whether they would go riding with their friends after school if their parents told them never to do that, there was a substantial positive relationship between self-reported delinquency and choosing to go with friends. A similar positive relationship was found between choosing to go with friends who were violating the law. We agree that those measures of peer commitment that involve some conflict element are probably tapping more than a single dimension of one's commitment to his or her friends. But the introduction of some social cost or risk associated with choosing to be with peers, or a forced choice between doing what friends or parents desire, does reflect a dimension of attachment or commitment that is relevant to the strength of one's bond to his or her friends. In this sense, such measures may be more comprehensive measures of peer commitment than that used by Hirschi (1969) and Krohn and Massey (1980).

In any event, for studies using measures of commitment involving no conflict element, the predominant finding is that there is no relationship between commitment to peers and delinquency. When measures incorporating some conflict element are used, there is a positive relationship between commitment to peers and delinquency. Neither conclusion is consistent with a pure control model; both are consistent with the integrated model.[8] Delinquent youths as compared to nondelinquent youths are equally or slightly more committed to their peer groups and are thus exposed to peer influences and socialization processes in these pro-delinquent groups to the same degree that nondelinquent youth are exposed to peer influences and socialization processes in conventional groups.

Selective recruitment and conditional influence of delinquent groups. The final issue involved in the proposed modification that considers bonding to both conventional and delinquent groups is the question of selective recruitment into delinquent groups and the conditional influence of socialization in delinquent groups. The first proposition is that delinquent groups are more likely to attract or recruit youths who are alienated from and only weakly bonded to conventional groups and activities. The second is that the effect of pro-delinquent group influences is mediated by the strength of one's bond to conventional groups and activities. In essence, the integrated model asserts that youths with strong bonds to conventional groups and activities are less likely to associate with delinquent peers and, if exposed to peers with this orientation, are less likely to be influenced by them.

A number of studies have found that attachment to delinquent peers is negatively related to attachment to parents, school, or conventional peers (Hirschi, 1969; Jensen, 1972; Jessor and Jessor, 1977; Elliott and Voss, 1974; Johnstone, 1981; Hindelang, 1973; Johnson, 1979; Toby and Toby, 1963). More direct evidence is provided by studies that have considered the impact of different patterns of bonding to both conventional and delinquent groups on delinquent behavior. Hirschi (1969) presents such an analysis, reporting the average number of self-reported delinquent acts for youth cross-classified by a stake in conformity index and number of delinquent friends. The stake in conformity index included measures of bonding to the school, parents, and conventional success goals. In this analysis, those with strong bonds to conventional groups and activities and weak attachment to deviant peers (i.e., no delinquent friends) had the lowest rates of self-reported delinquency; those with bonds to delinquent friends and a low stake in conformity had the highest rates of self-reported delinquency; and those with a low stake in conformity and no delinquent friends had relatively low to moderate rates of delinquency.[9] Finally, fewer than four percent of Hirschi's sample were classified as having both a high stake in conformity and bonds to delinquent friends; and those youth had lower rates of delinquency than those with the low conventional-high delinquent bonding pattern and higher rates than those in the low conventional-low delinquent bonding pattern.

These outcomes are precisely those anticipated by the integrated model and specified earlier in Figure 3.1. First, those with the highest rates of delinquency had low stakes in conformity and were bonded to delinquent peers. Also, these data indicate that the most delinquent youth were bonded youth; those with the weakest bonds (low stake in conformity and no delinquent friends) had low to moderate rates of delinquency. This latter pattern is the pattern predicted by a pure control model to be most conducive to delinquency. Not only were youth in the low stake-delinquent friend pattern more delinquent than these youth, but those in the *high stake*-delinquent friend pattern were also more delinquent. Second, virtually all boys with delinquent friends had low stakes in conformity. Although the temporal order is not clear, these results are consistent with a selective recruitment position. Third, the effect of bonding to delinquent peers on delinquency was conditioned by stake in conformity. Among those exposed to delinquent friends, boys with high stakes in conformity were less delinquent than were those with low stakes in conformity.

Linden and Hackler (1973) report on a study in which they used separate measures of attachment to conventional peers, deviant peers, and parents. They found that self-reported delinquency was inversely related to ties to parents and conventional peers, but positively related to ties to deviant peers. When they typed youth on the basis of high or low bonding to all three groups, those with high bonding to parents and conventional peers and weak bonding to delinquent peers had the lowest delinquency prevalence rate; those with low bonding to parents and conventional peers and high bonding to delinquent peers had the highest rate. In comparison, those with low bonding to all three groups had a moderate prevalence rate.[10] Again these findings are consistent with the integrated model; the most delinquent youth are bonded to delinquent friends, and the impact of delinquent friends is influenced by the level of bonding to parents and conventional peers. In some respects this analysis is more compelling than that of Hirschi's discussed earlier because measures of the strength of respondent's attachment to delinquent and nondelinquent friends were used rather than a report of the number of delinquent friends; i.e., a more direct measure of bonding to delinquent friends was used.

There are two additional studies that are similar to the Linden and Hackler study. Both have considered the interaction between conventional and deviant bonding relative to delinquency. Stanfield (1966) considered the interactive effects of father's discipline and involvement with delinquent peers on the prevalence of official conviction. The sample involved boys in the Cambridge-Somerville Youth Study (Witmer, 1951). Although a formal test for an interaction was not reported, the percentage convicted was highest (43 percent) for youth characterized by erratic or lax discipline and high involvement with delinquent peers. Among boys with high delinquent peer involvement and consistent family discipline, only 16 percent had convictions. Among those reporting low involvement with delinquent peers and either consistent or erratic/lax discipline, 14 and 23 percent, respectively, had convictions.[11] Stanfield concluded that there was an interactive effect present in these data; weak family controls (erratic or lax discipline) greatly increased the influence of delinquent companions. Again, the pattern of differences here are identical to those predicted in Figure 3.1.

Poole and Regoli (1979) report on a more formal test for interaction between an index of family support and a friend's self-reported delinquency. The dependent variable in the analysis was a measure of the respondent's self-reported delinquency. Employing a two-way analysis of variance test, they found significant main effects for both conventional and delinquent bonding measures and significant interaction effects on each of nine separate tests. Boys characterized by highly delinquent friends and low family supports reported an average of 30 offenses, compared to 6 for boys with highly delinquent friends and high family supports. As expected, the lowest rate of offending (M = 3.9) was found for boys reporting high family support and friends with low levels of reported delinquency. Youths with low family supports and friends with low delinquency rates reported an average of 9.5 offenses. Essentially the same pattern of relationships was observed when the measure of delinquency employed (for friend and respondent) was a variety or a seriousness measure. There is clear evidence here for the hypothesis that the relationship between bonding to delinquent peers and delinquency is conditioned by the level of bonding to conventional groups. Among those boys whose friends were highly involved in delinquency, the number of self-reported delinquent acts was over five times as great for those with low as compared to high levels of family support. The overall pattern of differences in this study was slightly different from that predicted in Figure 3.1, however. Contrary to our expectation, those boys characterized by low conventional and low delinquent bonding reported slightly higher rates of delinquent behavior than boys with high conventional and high delinquent bonding. However, delinquency rates for both groups were quite low compared to those for boys with low conventional and high delinquent bonding.

Although our focus on bonding to delinquent peers is not limited narrowly to bonding to delinquent gangs, Johnstone's (1983) study of gang recruiting and affiliation among black adolescents living in the Chicago Standard Metropolitan Statistical Area (SMSA) also supports the selective recruitment postulated in the integrated model. The opportunity to join a delinquent gang was related to the level of social disorganization in the neighborhood, and the decision to join a gang appeared to be governed by a boy's social and institutional attachments and self-definitions. Boys living in areas where delinquent gangs were active were able to resist recruiting efforts as long as they continued to believe in their chances of success as conventional adults.[12] Johnstone concludes:

> The data suggest that boys who fail at school and are rejected at home eventually come to see themselves as heading for failure as adults. It may be at this point that gangs become meaningful as alternative sources of attachment and commitment [Johnstone, 1983: 297].

Jessor and Jessor (1977) reported that those respondents in their study who valued peer opinions over those of their parents were more likely to (1) have friends who approved of delinquent behavior, (2) have friends who were involved in delinquent acts, and (3) be involved in delinquent acts themselves. This study is significant because it involves a different dimension of bonding (i.e., perceived influence of parents and peers on decision making) and the study was longitudinal and involved a true predictive analysis. In some respects, the measure of the relative strength of peer and parent influence resembles the measures of commitment containing some conflict element described earlier, and these findings are consistent with those reported for such measures; i.e., that bonding to peers is positively associated with delinquency. In any event, we may conclude from this study that those with stronger bonds to deviant than conventional groups were more likely to become involved in subsequent delinquent acts.

In another longitudinal study, Elliott and Voss (1974) report on subsequent rates of delinquency for youth initially classified by their commitment to peers and parents. The peer commitment measure involved a conflict element, choosing to be with friends even though these friends were "leading you into trouble."[13] Youths with initially high commitment to parents and low commitment to delinquent peers had the lowest rates of self-reported delinquency over the next three years (m = 4.48 offenses); those with an initially low commitment to parents and high commitment to delinquent peers had the highest subsequent delinquency rate (M = 9.98 offenses). Those with a low initial commitment to both parents and delinquent peers had a moderate rate of delinquency (M = 6.61) over the next three years.

In a change analysis that controlled for prior levels of self-reported delinquency, those with high parent-low delinquent peer commitment reported a relative decline in delinquency of approximately 1.3 offenses. Those with low parent-high delinquent peer commitment reported a relative increase of approximately 1 offense; those with low bonding to both parents and delinquent peers reported essentially no change in relative rates of delinquency over the next three years. Thus the only bonding category reporting an escalation of involvement in delinquency over time involved youths who reported an initially weak commitment to parents and a strong commitment to delinquent peers.

In both the simple incidence and the changing incidence analyses, youths who reported a high initial commitment to both parents and delinquent peers reported moderate rates of delinquency over time. In both cases, youths with this bonding pattern were more delinquent than those with low commitment to both parents and peers and less delinquent than those with a low commitment to parents and a high commitment to delinquent peers. Again, this set of outcomes is consistent with the modification proposed and inconsistent with a pure control model.

The Elliott and Voss (1974) data again confirm that the effect of bonding to delinquent peers on delinquency is influenced by simultaneous bonding to conventional groups (parents). Johnson (1979) and Johnstone (1981) report a similar finding, although their data are not longitudinal and involve no predictive analysis. In the Elliott and Voss (1974) analysis there was also evidence of a genuine interaction effect for parent and delinquent peer bonding on subsequent delinquency. Those with a low commitment to parents and a high commitment to delinquent peers had particularly high rates of delinquency over time, higher rates than could be accounted for by the independent direct effects of low parent and high delinquent peer bonding. Hirschi (1969) also notes an interaction effect for this same pattern (low stake in conformity and several delinquent friends).

SUMMARY

There is considerable support for each of the modifications suggested as necessary for an integration of control and learning theories. First, there is empirical support for direct socialization to delinquency. Among delinquent as compared to nondelinquent peers, the moral dimension of belief is perceived to be less salient for behavior; delinquent abilities and skills are positively valued; delinquent acts are perceived as normative in a statistical sense and approved of by friends; and delinquent behavior is more frequently modeled by friends. Although there are some exceptions involving particular dimensions of bonding, the evidence generally supports the position that delinquents are equally or more strongly bonded to their friends than are nondelinquents, and that these friends include delinquent youths. Delinquent youths have thus been exposed to pro-delinquent socialization experiences that should be as effective as the conventional socialization experiences provided by conventional groups.

Second, the major difference between those with high and low risks for delinquency lies not only in the strength of their bonds to other persons and groups, but also in the conventional or pro-delinquent orientations of those persons and groups to which they are bonded. The available evidence is consistent with the proposition that youths with weak bonds to conventional groups are more likely to be attracted to or recruited by delinquent groups although the temporal ordering of these variables has not been empirically established to our knowledge.

Finally, there is substantial research evidence that the influence of delinquent peer bonding on delinquent behavior is conditioned by the strength of bonds to conventional groups. Uniformly, youths with strong conventional and weak delinquent bonds have the lowest probability of delinquency, and youth with weak conventional and strong delinquent bonds have the highest probability of delinquency. In four of the studies reviewed there was evidence of a genuine interaction effect of conventional and delinquent group bonding on delinquency, demonstrating an unusually high vulnerability to delinquency on the part of youths with weak bonding to conventional groups and strong bonding to deviant groups. There was also evidence from longitudinal studies that supported the postulated temporal ordering of this relationship; i.e., that the pattern of conventional and delinquent bonding predicted future delinquency.

NOTES

1. We will use the term "delinquent group" to refer to groups of any size (small friendship clique to large gang) in which delinquent behavior is modeled and/or rein-

forced. Our use of this term does not imply homogeneity in delinquent acts across all members, nor does it imply that the group is organized specifically for delinquent activity.

2. Some attention has been given to the direct modeling effects of criminal parents and siblings (see Wootten, 1959; Ferguson, 1952; Glueck and Glueck, 1950; McCord et al., 1959; West, 1973; Severy, 1970; West and Farrington, 1977; Akers et al., 1979; Kandel et al., 1978; Jensen and Brownfield, 1983).

3. We are not equating social learning theory with cultural deviance theory. Kornhauser (1978) argues that a cultural deviance model presupposes a perfect, uniform socialization effectiveness and classifies Sutherland's theory of Differential Association as a cultural deviance theory. However, learning theorists do not assume a perfect socialization process (Akers, 1977; Rotter, 1954; Jessor and Jessor, 1977; Bandura, 1969), nor do we believe this is a fair characterization of Sutherland's Theory of Differential Association.

4. Reiss and Rhodes (1964) also noted that this dependence varied by type of delinquent act and social class. Although there was evidence of behavioral homophyly in these triads, Reiss and Rhodes concluded that close friendship choices were more closely associated with involvement in some form of delinquency than with specialization in specific types of delinquent activity. This conclusion is not inconsistent with a social learning or bonding to delinquent groups hypothesis, but does suggest that more than a simple modeling of specific behaviors is occurring. Our integrated model would lead us to expect that the beliefs and social reinforcements provided by delinquent groups would support a range of delinquent acts and that skill acquisition from modeling is a relatively minor aspect of the learning process in delinquent groups.

5. Unfortunately Hindelang used a dichotomy of his approval/disapproval scale for most of his analysis (indifferent, approved, and strongly approved versus disapprove and strongly disapprove), and he reports the percentages of youths who disapproved of each act for those committing and not committing each act. There is an obvious difference between perceiving that your friends are indifferent to delinquent acts and perceiving that they actually approve of them. However, Hindelang does report some overall percentages of youths in his study who "approve" of specific acts, and it is clear that a substantial percentage of these youths (10 to 35 percent for the offenses listed) responded that they approved of these acts. It is reasonable to assume that these percentages could be substantially higher for the subgroup reporting they committed these offenses and that the percentage reporting that their friends approved of these acts is as great or greater.

6. Although we have focused more upon peers and peer groups, it should be noted that there is also evidence that criminal parents and siblings may also provide social reinforcements for criminal behavior (Jessor and Jessor, 1977; Jessor, 1981; Knowles, 1979; Akers et al., 1979; West, 1973; Wootten, 1959; Ferguson, 1952; Glueck and Glueck, 1956; McCord et al., 1959).

7. The Phi Coefficient was calculated from Table No. 44, p. 146, dichotomizing the number of self-reported offenses into "none" and "one or more" and identification levels into "not at all" and "a few or most ways." Krohn and Massey (1980) report almost identical findings: The correlation (r) between peer attachment and nonserious delinquency was .00; with serious delinquency it was $-.10$; with drug use it was $-.03$.

8. Because the integrated model postulates that delinquent peers are the only persons and groups to which delinquent youth are strongly bonded, whereas

nondelinquent youth are bonded to their families, school, and conventional community groups (e.g., church, YM/WCA, etc.) as well as conventional peer groups, we may expect delinquents to have a slightly stronger bonding to their peers. Delinquents have a greater investment in their bonding to their adolescent friends, as they are likely to perceive little or no support from other groups and institutions.

9. Based upon the data in Hirschi (1969: 158, Table 52).

10. The finding that youths with low conventional bonding (to family and peers) and high bonding to delinquent peers reported higher levels of delinquent behavior than those with low bonding to all three groups is important in another respect. Hirschi and Gottfredson (1980), arguing from a pure control perspective, have asserted that the relationship between delinquent peer association and delinquent behavior reflects only an absence of peer restraints on delinquent behavior, not a reinforcement for delinquent acts. These data refute this claim. If bonding to delinquent peers involved only an absence of restraints on delinquency there should be no difference in the delinquency rates of these two groups. From a pure control perspective they both are characterized as having few restraints from either parents or peers. Yet the group with bonds to delinquent friends reports a higher involvement in delinquency, suggesting that involvement with delinquent friends involves more than an absence of peer restraints. Elliott (in press) reports a similar analysis and finding.

11. These percentages are based upon data presented in Table 5, collapsing high and low SES categories (Stanfield, 1966: 416). Stanfield reported that SES did influence the relationship of father's discipline and participation with delinquent peers on percentage convicted. He concluded that "SES intensifies the relationship of delinquency to parental rejection and discipline at *lower* levels. It intensifies the relationship of delinquency with the frequency of peer activitity at *higher* status levels" (1966: 417). Because SES is tangential to the issues of interest here, these findings are not discussed in the text.

12. Johnstone also found an association between having an official contact with the justice system and being recruited by a delinquent gang. He interprets this finding as indicating that gangs select new members from experienced delinquents rather than nondelinquents; i.e., that delinquency leads to being recruited by a gang. This particular causal ordering is consistent with a pure control perspective, but not with the integrated perspective. However, the temporal order of these two events is not controlled in the analysis, and it is just as plausible to interpret this finding in a way that is consistent with the integrated perspective (i.e., that recruitment leads to delinquency). Unfortunately, Johnstone does not present the data most critical to the support of one of these causal orderings over the other; whether those recruited (i.e., invited to join) but not becoming gang members had higher or lower delinquency rates than those with no gang contacts.

13. The parent commitment variable also involved a conflict element. The measure involved a three-item scale in which parents were chosen over friends and teachers as having the most influence (Elliott and Voss, 1974: 236).

4

The Fully Integrated Model

The fully integrated model incorporating all of the the modifications discussed earlier is presented in Figure 4.1, with the causal relationships identified by the solid arrows. This etiological sequence identifies strain, inadequate socialization, and social disorganization as the primary causes of weak bonding to conventional groups, activities, and norms. It further specifies that weak conventional bonding and/or high levels of strain lead some youths to seek out and become bonded to peer groups that provide positive reinforcements for and modeling of delinquent behavior; i.e., delinquent groups. And finally, it specifies that bonding to delinquent groups, when combined with weak bonding to conventional groups and norms, leads to a high probability of involvement in delinquent behavior. The line drawing in Figure 4.1 does not depict the conditional nature of the delinquent bonding-delinquent behavior relationship, but it is intended.

To facilitate our discussion of this model, we have also included pure strain and pure control paths in Figure 4.1, as indicated by broken arrows. In this case, the pure strain path refers to the direct effect of strain on delinquency; i.e., the effect of strain that is independent of conventional bonding and delinquent bonding. Likewise, the pure control path refers to the direct effect of weak controls on delinquency, given the other variables in the model.

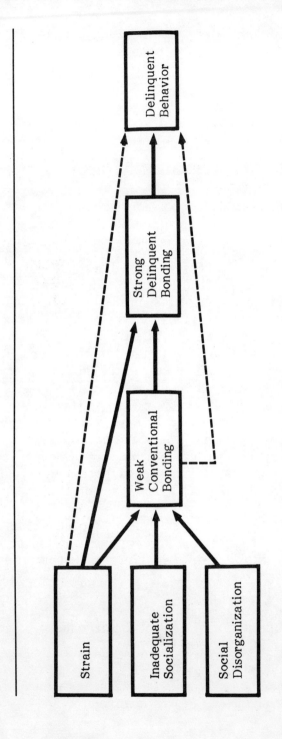

Figure 4.1 : The Integrated Model

CONCEPTUALIZATION AND
LOGICAL STRUCTURE

Before we turn to a review of the research evidence relative to the empirical claims of this model, several comments about the conceptualization and logical structure of the model are in order. First, we view the model as a modified social control-social disorganization model. Although the theoretical integration proposed here could probably be formulated with either social control or learning concepts, we have chosen to remain in the social control and social disorganization tradition and to employ the concepts and language of control theory. The primary justification for this choice is that control theory is a more general theoretical formulation that offers an explanation for criminal behavior at multiple levels of explanation. The use of this conceptual framework is thus in part an anticipation of our desire to extend the present integration to include social structural variables and system variables (secondary controls) that interface the primary social controls that are the focus of the present integration. This decision also reflects what is probably a disciplinary bias in the effort to achieve a healthy balance between individual variables and group or social context variables in the explanation for criminal behavior. A social control perspective places greater emphasis upon primary groups and institutional structures and practices when considering the interaction of the individual with his environment. The theory is thus more sociological than psychological in emphasis.

At a logical level, the integrated model involves an acknowledgement that there is variation in motivation for delinquency as well as variation in the restraints on delinquency, that there are factors that facilitate as well as restrain delinquency. The assertion that there is variation in motivation for delinquency is not new to the social disorganization tradition as this is the central variable in strain theories. Both sources of variation are thus found within the social disorganization tradition. For example, Shaw and McKay (1942) and Thrasher (1927) included both sources of variation in their explanations of delinquency; both weak conventional controls and exposure to the influence of delinquent companions or groups were postulated causes of delinquency. The proposed model thus lies within a single theoretical tradition although it includes sources of variation that have been emphasized more strongly in other theoretical traditions.

We also employed the concepts and language of social disorganization and control theory to avoid confusion between the explanation of delinquency proposed here and that proposed by differential association theory (Sutherland, 1947). Differential association is a type of social learning theory that has been tied historically to the cultural deviance tradition and subcultural explanations for crime (Kornhauser, 1978; Hirschi, 1979; Hirschi and Gottfredson, 1980). There are certainly some similarities between the model we have proposed and a differential association model, but the two models differ in the following ways: (1) the integrated model does not require or depend upon the presence of a delinquent subculture; (2) differential association postulates that all group effects on behavior are mediated by their influence on personal attitudes toward the law, whereas the integrated model considers belief in the legal norms as only one dimension of bonding and only one type of control on behavior; and (3) differential association assumes a relatively passive actor and an unconditional learning process, whereas the integrated model specifies an active selection/recruitment into delinquent groups and a conditional influence of such groups upon behavior.

A second comment on the structure of the integrated model concerns the direct effects of strain and control on delinquency. Although not denying the possibility of these direct effects, we believe they will be quite small as compared to that of the major path specified in the model. Each of these paths involves a single source of variation, either variation in restraints or in perceived opportunities for achieving valued goals. We hypothesized in our earlier description of this integrated model (Elliott et al., 1979) that the strain path is likely to involve occasional delinquent acts or a temporary pattern of criminal behavior rather than a sustained pattern. This is because there are no social supports for delinquency in this etiological path and a prolonged involvement in delinquency substantially increases the risk of discovery, which places the offender's stake in conventional groups and activities in jeopardy. We also postulate that the direct control path involves an occasional as opposed to a sustained pattern of delinquency because there are no group supports or rewards for this behavior. Further, given the findings of Meade and Marsden (1981) and Krohn and Massey (1980) presented earlier, it appears that a pure control path may account for some trivial, minor violations but has little or no explanatory power for serious delinquent behavior (see also Aultman, 1979, and Johnstone, 1981). These two paths are expected to account for a small part of the variance in total delinquency as measured at a given point in time, but little or no variance in sustained delinquency that reflects a pattern of delinquency covering longer periods of time.

Third, the model is not fully specified. There are two intervening variables in the model: Conventional bonding and delinquent bonding. The model does identify the major causes of weak conventional bonding as specified by control theorists; i.e., strain, inadequate socialization, and social disorganization. The causes of bonding to delinquent groups, however, are not fully specified. The model does identify high levels of strain and weak bonding to conventional groups and activities as conditions leading youths to develop bonds to delinquent groups. However, youths may become bonded to delinquent groups for other reasons as well; i.e., as a result of residential location, shared interests, common activities or tasks, and other selective social processes. These causes are not identified in the model. This does not pose a problem for the explanation of delinquency because the causal connection between bonding to delinquent peers and delinquency is postulated to hold only for those with weak conventional bonds. It does mean that in our test of this model we do not expect to account for a high proportion of the variation in bonding to delinquent groups.

Finally, the model in Figure 4.1 is primarily a sequential model with bonding to delinquent groups as the most proximate cause of delinquent behavior. This ordering is based upon the chronological ordering of a youth's involvement in the major socialization settings (i.e., the family, the school, and peer groups) and changes in the relative influence of these socialization agents/contexts over the course of the life span. Those most vulnerable to recruitment by delinquent groups or most likely to choose delinquent friends are those with preexisting weak bonds to the family, school and conventional norms and activities. Those experiencing strain (with or without an attenuation of social controls) are also postulated to be more susceptible to delinquent group influences. But the only direct cause of delinquency is a differential reinforcement for delinquency resulting from bonding to a delinquent group. In a pure sequential model the causal influence of the most proximate cause absorbs the entire effect of all of the more distal causes. However, given the conditional relationship postulated, the model is not a simple sequential model. Although conventional bonding and deviant bonding are ordered sequentially, it is the joint effect of prior weak conventional controls and current group reinforcements for delinquency that causes delinquency. This is an important structural aspect of the proposed model because it is by virtue of this postulated conditional relationship that the model holds some promise for improved predictive efficiency over the pure forms of the theories involved in the integration.

EMPIRICAL SUPPORT

We have previously reviewed much of the research evidence related to particular relationships specified in the integrated model. Although the evidence has been limited and far from conclusive in some instances, it has been generally consistent with the empirical claims of the model. Our focus here is upon two final issues: (1) the research evidence relative to the claim that the direct effects of conventional bonding and strain are weak and that the influence of these variables is mediated by bonding to delinquent peers and (2) the question of the correct temporal ordering of the variables in the model. We have already considered the evidence for the other critical claim of the model that there is an interaction between conventional and delinquent bonding.

The research to date clearly establishes that association, attachment, commitment,and other dimensions of bonding to delinquent friends are related to involvement in delinquent behavior and drug use (Glueck and Glueck, 1950; Cressey, 1952, 1953; Short, 1957, 1960; Glaser, 1960; Reiss and Rhodes, 1964; Voss, 1964; Erickson and Empey, 1965; Lerman, 1968; Hirschi, 1969; Jensen, 1972; Hindelang, 1973; West, 1973; Elliott and Voss, 1974; Knight and West, 1975; Conger, 1976; Jensen and Eve, 1976; Jensen and Erickson, 1978; Jessor and Jessor, 1977; Meier and Johnson, 1977; West and Farrington, 1977; Brennan et al., 1978; Ginsberg and Greenley, 1978; Kandel, 1978; Akers et al., 1979; Johnson, 1979; Figueira-McDonough et al., 1981; Hindelang et al., 1981; Meade and Marsden, 1981; Gottfredson, 1982; Matsueda, 1982; Thompson et al., 1982; La Grange and White, 1983). More importantly, multivariate studies employing a delinquent peer bonding measure together with conventional bonding measures have nearly always found the delinquent peer measure to be the strongest single predictor of delinquency. The significance of this uniformity in research findings is that it provides some empirical support for the causal ordering of conventional and delinquent bonding variables specified in the integrated model; i.e., the pattern of relationships is such that delinquent bonding can logically mediate the total influence of conventional bonding, whereas the reverse is not true (Blalock, 1964; Kornhauser, 1978). Bonding to delinquent peers appears to be a more proximate cause of delinquency than is bonding to conventional groups and norms.[1]

If we tentatively accept this causal ordering for our explanatory model, the critical empirical question is then whether strain and conventional bonding have any substantial impact on delinquent behavior once the influence of bonding to delinquent peers is removed. The integrated model asserts that independent effects of strain and conventional bonding will be nonexistent or very small; i.e., that any significant effects of these variables will be mediated by bonding to delinquent peers. A number of studies provides evidence relative to this issue; i.e.; they involve analyses in which the influence of bonding to delinquent peers is controlled or removed so that the independent effects of conventional bonding and/or strain on delinquency can be determined.

Hirschi (1969) examined the simultaneous effects of stakes in conformity (attachment to parents, attachment to school, and commitment to conventional achievement) and delinquency of companions on delinquent behavior. He reports that all of the conventional bonding variables were related to delinquency when controlling for the delinquency of one's companions. In an independent analysis of Hirschi's data (The Richmond Youth Study), Jensen (1972) found that paternal supervision and emotional support were significantly related to delinquency while holding the number of delinquent friends constant. The number of delinquent friends was clearly the strongest independent predictor in both analyses; controlling for this variable substantially reduced the magnitude of the relationship between conventional bonding and delinquency, but conventional bonding did have a significant effect upon delinquency that was independent of the number of delinquent friends. However, the magnitude of this independent effect was weak in both analyses (r =.14 or gamma =−.28).

Both Jensen and Eve (1976) and Linden (1978) report on a multiple regression analysis involving the Richmond Youth Study data in which the independent effects of conventional and delinquent bonding measures could be compared. The Jensen and Eve study involved the total sample and the combination of six measures of conventional bonding and a measure of association with delinquent friends. The total set of predictors accounted for 27 percent of the variance in self-reported delinquency for whites and for 15 percent of the variance for blacks. The Linden study involved only white males and the combination of three conventional bonding measures (parental support, finishing homework, and skipping school) and a measure of association with delinquent peers as predictors of self-reported delinquency. This set of predictors accounted for

38 percent of the variance in delinquency.[2] In both cases the measure of association with delinquent peers was the strongest individual predictor, but conventional bonding predictors made substantial independent contributions to the total explained variance. In the Linden study the three conventional bonding measures accounted for an additional 11 percent in explained variance once the effect of delinquent peer associations was removed. In both studies, there were moderate independent effects of conventional bonding measures on delinquency.

Simons et al. (1980) tested a mixed theoretical model on a statewide sample of Iowa teenagers. The multiple regression analysis included two measures of strain (education and occupational), two measures of conventional bonding (parental rejection and alienation from norms), two measures of negative labeling (parental rejection and alienation from norms), and a measure of differential association (normative orientations of friends). Each of these predictors made a significant independent contribution to the explained variance (no R^2 given). However, the effects of strain measures are extremely weak (beta weights $= -.08$ and $.04$); and the effects of conventional bonding and labeling are only slightly stronger (beta weights ranging from $.08$ to $.15$). Again the differential association measure was the strongest predictor (beta weight $= .35$) in the analysis.

Johnstone (1981) tested a causal model that included five predictors of delinquency: (1) neighborhood affluence; (2) family SES; (3) perceived opportunities for crime; (4) family integration; and (5) attachment to delinquent peers. The family integration measure was a composite of measures of attachment to parents, shared activity in the family, the extent to which parents set rules, and respect for parental authority. The general model accounted for 28 percent of the variance in self-reported delinquency. With regard to the effects of particular variables, attachment to delinquent peers accounted for the vast majority of the explained variance in delinquent behavior whereas the effect of family integration was relatively weak (betas of $.422$ and $-.156$, respectively). The analysis also indicated that the effect of family integration was partially mediated by attachment to delinquent peers. When the effect of delinquent peers was removed, the remaining portion of the total explained variance attributable to the combined effect of family integration, neighborhood affluence, SES, and perceived opportunities for crime was less than 5 percent. Further, the path coefficients for the remaining variables suggest that family integration has about the same relative influence on delinquency as the remaining three measures. Taken together, these findings indicate a statistically significant independent influence of family integration upon delinquency but one that is very weak, contributing relatively little to the overall explanation of delinquency.

Johnson (1979) also tested a rather complex causal model incorporating ten predictors of delinquent behavior. Included in this set of predictors were several conventional bonding measures (e.g., love/concern of parent for child, attachment to parents, success in school performance, attachment to school) and delinquent bonding measures (e.g., delinquent friends and delinquent values). The results of a path analysis revealed several findings relative to our concern about the effects of conventional bonding measures once the effect of bonding to delinquent peers had been removed. For males, there was no direct effect of attachment to parents, love/concern of parent, or attachment to school on self-reported delinquent behavior. The only conventional bonding measure with a direct influence on delinquency was school performance. The effects of the other conventional bonding measures were indirect, mediated by the delinquent bonding measures. The only conventional bonding measure with a direct effect upon delinquency for females was attachment to school. All of the other conventional bonding measures exerted indirect influences on delinquency through attachment to school or delinquent friends. In this study, bonding to parents was not significantly related to delinquency for either males or females. For both, there was a significant direct effect of one of the two school bonding measures. Although a precise estimate of the independent predictive power of school bonding variables was not provided, the path coefficients again indicate that these measures were weak predictors compared to the delinquent friends measure.

Meade and Marsden (1981) tested an explanatory model that integrated social control, strain, and differential association perspectives with data from a statewide sample of Illinois youth. This model included a composite measure of conventional bonding (involvement and identification with parents, school, and religion), a composite measure of strain (perceived achievement chances), a norm attenuation measure (perceived tolerance for deviant acts), and a measure of attachment to delinquent peers. Although norm attenuation is treated as a separate theoretical construct in this analysis, it may be considered a measure of the belief dimension of conventional bonding. Three measures of delinquency were used as dependent variables in a causal modeling analysis: Theft-violence, drug use, and status offenses.

Attachment to delinquent peers was the strongest correlate of delinquency, regardless of which measure of delinquency was employed. The strength of strain and conventional bonding predictors was similar when the theft-violence scale was the measure of delinquency, but the conventional bonding predictor was stronger than the strain predictor for the other two measures of delinquency.

The causal modeling analysis revealed that for all measures of delinquency the primary explanatory variable was attachment to delinquent peers. When the criterion was the theft-violent measure of delinquency, both strain and conventional bonding (including norm attenuation) were only weakly predictive of delinquency. Over 23 percent of the variance in theft-violent behavior was explained by attachment to delinquent peers while the remaining strain and conventional bonding measures combined accounted for an additional 3.8 percent of the variance. This analysis also revealed that the effects of conventional bonding were partially mediated by attachment to delinquent peers. The effect of strain, on the other hand, was not mediated by attachment to delinquent peers.

For both drug use and status offense measures of delinquency, conventional bonding measures again had a weak
independent effect upon delinquency. The predictive power of
conventional bonding was greater for status offenses than for
drug use or theft-violence offenses, but was still weak relative
to that for attachment to delinquent peers. There was no
significant direct effect of strain on either drug use or status
offense measures. In both cases, strain had weak indirect
effects on delinquency through conventional bonding and
attachment to delinquent peers.

Although the specific linkages proposed and the conceptualization of variables are clearly different, the Meade and
Marsden study does include measures appropriate for a general
test of the integrated model proposed here by considering the
direct and indirect effects of all three major variables in a single
causal model. In this sense, the analysis presents particularly
important evidence relative to the empirical claims of the
integrated model. The findings are generally consistent with
these claims: Bonding to delinquent peers accounts for the vast
majority of the explained variance in delinquent behavior; the
effects of strain and conventional bonding are at least partially
mediated by bonding to delinquent peers; and direct effects of
these variables are small or nonsignificant.

A very similar set of findings are reported by Gottfredson
(1982) and LaGrange and White (1983) in tests of mixed
social control-differential association models using path
analysis. Gottfredson reports that the effects of conventional
bonding measures (educational expectations, beliefs, attachment to school, attachment to parents) are largely indirect,
mediated by the pro-delinquent influences of friends. Only
attachment to parents had a direct effect on delinquency, and
that was relatively weak (beta $= -.118$). The general model
accounted for 32 percent of the variation in delinquent behavior;
virtually all of this explained variance was attributable to the
measure of pro-delinquent influences of friends (beta $= .458$).
The only other significant direct effect involved a measure of
negative parental role modeling (beta $= .096$). Gottfredson
also notes that three of the four conventional bonding measures

were more strongly associated with pro-delinquent peer influences than with delinquent behavior, a finding that is consistent with the postulated causal order of the independent variables in the integrated model.

The test by LaGrange and White (1983) produced a similar level of explained variance in delinquency (36 percent). Five measures of conventional bonding were used (perceived parental love, attachment to parents, school performance, school attachment, and commitment to education). The proportion of friends who engaged in various delinquent acts was used as a measure of delinquent associates. Neither parental love nor school attachment had a significant direct effect on self-reported delinquency. The path coefficients for the remaining conventional bonding measures were weak to moderate in size (.128, .138, and .198 as ordered above). This analysis indicated that much of the influence of weak family and school bonding was mediated by delinquent companions, although there were weak independent effects of family bonding and a moderate independent effect of school bonding. Again, delinquent companions was by far the strongest predictor (beta = .405) of delinquent behavior.

Patterson and Dishion (1984) report on a test of mixed social control-social learning model using a structural modeling analysis (LISREL). Three constructs, parental monitoring of youth, academic skills, and deviant peers together accounted for 54 percent of the variation in delinquency (based on self-report and police contact indicators). The influence of academic skills was moderate and direct; the influence of parental monitoring was both direct and indirect (mediated by delinquent peers). It was also the case that two constructs, parental monitoring and social skills (hostile/withdrawn, interpersonal competence, and self-ratings), accounted for 80 percent of the variance in the delinquent peer association construct. The model thus postulates that inadequate monitoring by parents and poor social skills leads to association with delinquent peers, and together with poor academic performance and inadequate monitoring by parents, leads to delinquent behavior. Patterson and Dishion report an adequate fit between this

model and the observed covariance structure. Although the
direct effects of parental monitoring and academic performance constructs are stronger than postulated in the integrated
model, the results of this analysis are otherwise very consistent
with the proposed integrated model.

Several additional studies focusing upon marijuana and
alcohol use also provide estimates of the effects of strain and
conventional bonding when combined with deviant bonding.
Meier and Johnson (1977) report the results of a multiple
regression analysis involving 16 predictors of marijuana use.
These predictors were organized into four conceptual sets: (1)
social background; (2) legal sanctions (perceived certainity
and severity of punishment and knowledge of the law); (3)
number of friends using marijuana;[3] and (4) respondent attitudes (belief that marijuana use is an immoral activity and fear
of marijuana use). Both the perceptions of legal sanctions and
respondent attitude sets can be construed as measures of the
belief dimension of conventional bonding. The study sample
involved adults (aged 18 and over) living in Cook County,
Illinois, a subset of participants in a 1971 national drug survey
(Abelson et al., 1972).

The total set of 16 predictors accounted for 72 percent of the
variance in marijuana use in this sample. Once the influence of
the friends using marijuana measure was removed, the remaining variables accounted for an additional 6 percent of explained
variance. Given that the social background variable set was a
substantially stronger predictor than either the perceived legal
sanctions or respondent attitudes set (when considered alone),
it appears that the two conventional bonding sets contribute
relatively little to the explanation of marijuana use in this
sample.

Winfree et al. (1981) investigated the impact of peer support
for drug use, parental social support, attitudes toward the law,
and age and sex on the use of marijuana and alcohol. The
sample involved approximately 600 students in a rural school
district. The findings from a multiple regression analysis were
presented separately for Caucasians and Native Americans.
With regard to drug use among Caucasians, the total explained

variance in marijuana use was 41 percent, with peer support for drug use accounting for 28 percent of the variance. The remaining variables accounted for an additional 13 percent of explained variance. The total explained variance in alcohol use was 27 percent, with peer support accounting for 21 percent of the variance. The combined effect of the remaining variables was thus 6 percent.

For Native Americans, total explained variance in marijuana use was 47 percent, with peer support accounting for 30 percent and the other variables an additional 17 percent. Considered alone, age/sex was the strongest predictor among the remaining variables (R^2 = .223), followed by parental support (R^2 = .118) and attitudes toward the law (R^2 = .042). Peer support accounted for virtually all of the explained variance (15 percent) in alcohol use by Native Americans, the remaining variables accounting for less than a one percent increase.

Akers and Cochran (1983) compared the empirical support for strain, social control, and social learning theories as independent models accounting for adolescent marijuana use. They also considered the independent contributions of each theory in a combined mixed model. The study involved over 3000 youths in grades 7 to 12 in seven midwestern communities. When examined individually, they found that the learning model accounted for 68 percent of the variance in marijuana use; control theory accounted for 30 percent of the variance; and strain theory accounted for 3 percent. When all measues were included in a single model, 69 percent of the variance in marijuana use was explained. The mixed model thus generated only a marginal improvement in explained variance over the social learning model. Further, in the single multiple regression including the total set of predictors, all strain and social control predictors had essentially zero beta weights. Akers and Cochran then selected the strongest four predictors from both the strain and social control sets and the three strongest predictors from the social learning set, and reran the multiple regression analysis. Again, the only predictors producing beta weights of .10 or larger were the three social learning predictors. The explained variance in this test was 67 percent. The three predictors accounting for this level of explained variance were differential peer associations (beta = .442), friends reaction to marijuana use (beta = .154), and positive/negative definitions of use (beta = .237).

All of the above studies involve cross-sectional designs. As a result, the tests are not genuine predictive tests and may inflate the true causal significance of some or all of the predictor variables in the model because cause and effect relationships are confounded (Elliott and Voss, 1974; Kandel et al., 1978).[4] Fortunately there are several longitudinal studies that have examined the realtionships between these variables and delinquency and drug use.

Kandel et al. (1978) reported on a longitudinal study of the interpersonal influences of parents and peers upon initiation into drug use. This study involved a two-wave panel of high school students in New York State during the 1971-1972 academic year. Four variable clusters obtained at the beginning of the academic year were used as predictors of initiation into drug use that occurred at some point during the academic year. The four variable clusters were: (1) parental influences, (parental behavior, attitudes and values, and quality of parent-adolescent relationship); (2) peer influences (peer behavior, attitudes and values, quality of subject-best friend relationship, and drug availability); (3) subjects' values and beliefs; and (4) subjects' prior involvement in delinquent behavior and drug use. The variance explained by each cluster alone and the increments of additional variance explained by each cluster in a stepwise multiple regression analysis were determined. Three stages of initiation were considered: Initiation into the use of hard liquor, initiation into the use of marijuana, and initiation into the use of other illicit drugs.

The total explained variance due to peer influences, parental influences, and beliefs-values was 12 percent for initiation into hard liquor use, 18 percent for initiation into marijuana use, and 25 percent for initiation into other illicit drug use.[5] When the effect of peer influences was removed, parental influences and beliefs-values accounted for an additional 3 percent in explained variance for initiation into hard liquor use, a 7 percent increase in explained variance for initiation into marijuana use, and a 15 percent increase in explained variance for other illicit drug use. The additional effects of parent bonding and conventional beliefs were thus small for initiation into hard liquor use but substantial for initiation into other illicit drug use. It was also the case that parental and peer influences were essentially independent influences in this analysis; i.e., there was little evidence for an effect of parental influences through peer influences. A substantial part of the influence of beliefs-values, on the other hand, did appear to be operating through parental and/or peer influences.

Ginsberg and Greenley (1978) compared the predictive utility of the following measures: (1) attachment to delinquent (drug using) peers; (2) attachment to conventional social institutions (political, religious, and economic); (3) involvement in schoolwork and conventional activities and organizations; and (4) psychological stress (e.g., anxiety, loneliness, depression) in a longitudinal study of marijuana use. The subjects were a probability sample of students registered at the University of Wisconsin—Madison in the fall of 1971 (Time 1) who also participated in a follow-up questionnaire administered in the winter of 1974 (Time 2). The analyses involved multiple regression and path analysis, estimating the effect of Time 1 predictors on subsequent marijuana use, controlling for Time 1 marijuana use.

The measure of attachment to delinquent peers was again the strongest single predictor of marijuana use, whether considering cross-sectional or lagged relationships. Involvement in conventional activities and organizations was unrelated to marijuana use at either Time 1 or Time 2. Commitment to conventional institutions and psychological stress were related to marijuana use at both time periods. In the predictive analysis, the only measures having any direct effect upon marijuana use were marijuana use at Time 1 and attachment to deviant peers at Time 1. Together these two variables accounted for 44 percent of the explained variance in marijuana use at Time 2. With prior marijuana use and attachment to deviant peers controlled, neither of the conventional bonding measures nor the psychological stress measure was significantly related to marijuana use at Time 2. In a separate analysis predicting use or nonuse of marijuana at Time 2 for those subjects reporting no use at Time 1, attachment to deviant peers was again the only significant predictor of initiation into marijuana use. The conventional bonding measures in this study had no independent causal influence on either initiation into marijuana use or changes in level of use over time.

In a longitudinal study of delinquency, Elliott and Voss (1974) predicted the change in level of self-reported delinquency between junior and senior high school years with a set of predictors that included both strain and conventional bonding measures, as well as measures of bonding to delinquent peers.[6] Both origin (ninth grade) and change scores (ninth to twelfth grades) for each predictor were included in a stepwise multiple regression analysis. Unfortunately, the predictors were treated as individual variables and not introduced into the stepwise analysis as variable sets or in any predetermined order. Separate analyses were completed for males and females.

The level of total explained variance was similar for both sexes (21 percent), and commitment to delinquent peers (gain score) was the strongest predictor for both.[7] Traditional measures of strain contributed no significant increase in explained variance. In fact, had these measures entered the stepwise analysis first, they would have accounted for less than one percent of the explained variance in the change in delinquency over time. The relationship between strain and prior delinquency was slightly stronger, but these measures had essentially no predictive power. Conventional bonding measures, on the other hand, made significant contributions to the prediction of delinquency. Although the exact increase in explained variance for the set of bonding variables was not presented, it was approximately 10 percent for both sexes.

The simple (zero order) and multiple correlations between predictors and prior delinquency were uniformly stronger than the relationships with future delinquency or the change in delinquency (controlling for prior delinquency). This finding suggests that cross-sectional studies do promote inflated estimates of the predictive power of these variables, but in this case the relative power of strain, conventional bonding, and deviant bonding measures was quite similar regardless of the time location of the delinquency measure.

A final longitudinal study providing evidence on the predictive power of conventional bonding and deviant bonding measures is that of Jessor and Jessor (1977). The theoretical model tested was a social learning model that incorporated a set of personality predictors and a set of perceived environment predictors. The former included several measures that have been used as internal control measures, e.g., expectations for academic achievement and tolerance for deviance (commitment to conventional norms); and the latter included measures of external controls (e.g., parental support, parental controls, friends approval) and friends' modeling of deviance. Criterion measures used in a series of stepwise multiple regression analyses included a General Deviance Scale, marijuana use, and a Multiple Problem Behavior Index (a composite measure that included problem drinking, marijuana use, nonvirginity, activism, and a set of delinquent acts).

A general test of the model incorporating the strongest individual predictor variables from each of the six conceptual domains in the personality and perceived environment variable sets (designated as a field test) produced a total explained variance on the General Deviance scale of 45-46 percent (male-female); for marijuana use the explained variance was 42-46 percent; and for the Multiple Problem Behavior Index it was 52-55 percent. When the influence of friends' modeling of deviance was removed, the remaining variables in the analysis accounted for 19-26 percent of the explained variance in General Deviance; 9 percent of the explained variance in marijuana use; and 8-10 percent of the explained variance in the Multiple Problem Behavior Index.

In sum, the above review of both cross-sectional and longitudinal studies testing the relative strength of predictor variables in mixed causal models is generally supportive of the empirical claims of the proposed integrated model. Measures of bonding to delinquent peers are clearly the strongest individual predictors of delinquency and drug use. Further, although there are exceptions, the pattern of relationships is generally consistent with the claim that bonding to delinquent groups mediates a substantial part of the total influence of strain and conventional bonding on delinquent behavior. This claim is less well supported in drug studies.

Strain appears to have little or no independent causal influence on delinquency or drug use; any significant influence appears to be weak and/or indirect, mediated by weak conventional bonding and/or bonding to delinquent peers. However, relatively few studies incorporated both strain and bonding to delinquent peers measures, and any conclusions about the independent effects of strain on delinquency and drug use may be premature.

The findings relative to the independent effects of conventional bonding measures on delinquency and drug use are mixed. Several studies found no significant effects once the influence of attachment to delinquent peers was removed; others found significant but weak effects; and still others found that these measures had a substantial influence on delinquency or drug use. Because these differences were found among the longitudinal as well as the cross-sectional studies, these findings must be viewed as equivocal on this issue.

TEMPORAL ORDER

The final issue to be addressed concerns the temporal ordering of the variables in the model. We have argued earlier that the family and school are nearly always conventional socializing agencies and that the earliest exposure to pro-delinquent influences typically occurs in peer groups, usually during early adolescence when the peer group influence comes to compete with that of parents and teachers. From a historical perspective then, one's earliest experiences are in predominantly pro-social contexts, and for most persons, exposure to pro-delinquent influences doesn't occur until late childhood or early adolescence. On these grounds we have postulated that involvement with and commitment to delinquent peers is the most proximate cause of delinquency and drug use and mediates the influence of weak bonding to parents, school, and conventional norms. We also believe that there is some limited empirical support for the view that weak conventional bonding leads to bonding to delinquent peers that, in turn, leads to delinquent behavior (cited earlier). Clearly the size of the zero-order relationships of delinquent peers with delinquency and conventional bonds with delinquency indicates that if one of these predictors mediates the influence of the other, it is delinquent peers that mediate conventional bonds.

Although we believe this causal ordering is the most plausible, it may not be critical to the major empirical claim of the integrated model because we postulate that the delinquent peer-delinquency relationship is conditioned by conventional bonding. It is the joint occurrence of weak conventional bonds and bonds to delinquent peers that causes a frequent and sustained involvement in delinquency. Which occurs first may not be critical because both are required. It is thus possible for a person to acquire delinquent friends before his or her bonds to family, school, and conventional norms become attenuated. We are not claiming that this is the typical ordering, but that either ordering may be consistent with the claims of the integrated model.

The critical temporal ordering issue is whether bonding to delinquent peers, the most proximate variable in the causal model, precedes or follows delinquent behavior. A number of researchers have argued that attachment and commitment to delinquent peers may be an effect of delinquency rather than a cause (Hirschi, 1969; Gould, 1969; Kornhauser, 1978; Hirschi and Gottfredson, 1980). These two possible causal orderings of the delinquent bonding-delinquent behavior relationship have become known as the "feathering" and the "flocking" hypotheses, and Hirschi viewed the task of determining the relative validity of these two hypotheses "the key theoretical problem in the field of delinquency" (1969: 159). Fortunately, there is some empirical evidence that bears upon this question.

The longitudinal studies reviewed above provide direct evidence for the association between bonding to delinquent peers and delinquency with the temporal order of these variables controlled. These data thus provide supportive evidence for a causal relationship between bonding to delinquent peers and delinquency. They do not, of course, allow us to reject the claim that delinquency also leads to delinquent bonding or the claim that delinquent behavior has a stronger impact on the selection of one's peer group than the reverse. Nonetheless the consistency of the predictive power of the bonding to deviant peer measures over different samples, different periods of follow-up (ranging from less than nine months to over three years), and for initiation into delinquency and drug use, as well as changing involvement in delinquency and drug use, provides impressive evidence in support of the claim that bonding to deviant peers is a cause of subsequent delinquency and drug use. It is important to remember, however, that verification of the causal role of bonding to delinquent peers does not logically require the rejection of the claim that delinquent behavior leads one to acquire delinquent friends, nor does it require the delinquent friends-delinquent behavior relationship to be the stronger of the two relationships.

More direct evidence on the relative strength of the alternative causal orderings of these two variables is provided by two studies that compared group selection and group socialization influences as determinants of drug use homogeneity within adolescent groups. Both Cohen (1977) and Kandel (1978) established group affiliation at two points in time on the basis of sociometric choice data. Using these longitudinal data on group membership, they examined how joiners and leavers influenced group homogeneity in drug use and how individual changes while in the group influenced group homogeneity in drug use.

Both studies concluded that selection and socialization were reciprocal processes; i.e., homogeneity in drug use behavior was achieved both by socialization processes within the group and by the selection/termination of group members over time. In the Cohen study, selection appeared to be the stronger influence. The Kandel study involved a much larger sample, dyads as compared to larger group structures and a more sophisticated data analysis, and in this study socialization appeared to be of slightly greater importance in generating group homogeneity in drug use behavior. In both studies, the short time lag over which these effects were examined probably resulted in an underestimation of socialization as compared to selection influences because the former requires interaction over an extended period, whereas the latter may not. In any case, both studies confirm that attachment to deviant peers and involvement in delinquent and drug use behavior are reciprocal processes; bonding to delinquent and/or drug-using groups does lead to the initiation of those behaviors; and the use of drugs does increase the likelihood of one's joining a drug-using group.

Given the strong evidence for group homogeneity in behavior, involving both selection/termination and socialization process, bonding to delinquent groups takes on particular importance when attempting to account for a sustained involvement in delinquency or drug use. Kandel notes:

> Adolescents coordinate their choices of friends and their behavior . . . so as to maximize congruency within the friendship pair. If there is a state of imbalance such that the friend's attitude or behavior is incongruent with the adolescent's, the adolescent will either break off the friendship and seek another friend or will keep the friend and modify his own drug behavior [1978: 433-435].

Both the Cohen and Kandel studies provide evidence of strong group pressures for behavioral congruence. Under these circumstances, it would be extremely difficult for an adolescent to maintain a delinquent or drug use behavior pattern while continuing his or her membership in a conventional peer group that rejected or disapproved of this behavior.

In the longitudinal study of marijuana use by Ginsberg and Greenley (1978), these researchers noted that attachment to drug-using peers at Time 1 predicted marijuana use at Time 2 only sightly better than marijuana use at Time 1 predicted attachment to drug-using peers at Time 2. They concluded that

the attachment to drug-using peers and marijuana use relationship was a reciprocal causal relationship of approximately
equal strength. They pursued this relationship further through
a sixteenfold table analysis. Lazarsfield's (1973) index of
mutual effect confirmed that the causal influence of each
variable was approximately equal. They then calculated
Kessler's (1977) indices for generating and preserving effects
and found that both variables had primarily generating effects
(producing increases rather than decreases in the other variable) and that neither was causally dominant.

SUMMARY

It must be acknowledged that none of these analyses actually
demonstrates a causal relationship between bonding to delinquent peers and subsequent delinquent behavior. What is
demonstrated is that this variable continues to be strongly
associated with delinquency when the hypothesized temporal
order is imposed upon the data. Knowledge about bonding to
delinquent peers does allow one to more accurately predict
future initiation into and changing involvement in delinquent
behavior and drug use.

These data also support the position that bonding to delinquent groups and delinquent behavior are mutually reinforcing
variables with approximately equal influence on each other.
The association between bonding to delinquent peers and
delinquency/drug use as established in cross-sectional studies
thus reflects both socialization and selection processes, both
causes and effects of delinquency. It is reasonable to assume,
therefore, that these cross-sectional associations overestimate
the causal influence of bonding to delinquent peers. At the
same time, the traditional causal claim can not be rejected on
the grounds that the association is entirely or even primarily
the result of delinquent behavioral influences upon bonding
patterns. Those studies that control the temporal order of these
variables indicate that bonding to deviant peers continues to be
the best predictor of delinquency.

The consistency of findings involving different populations, different measures of theoretical constructs, and different forms of analysis is impressive. In addition, the covergence of findings from studies of the relationship between delinquent peer bonding and delinquent behavior with those from studies of selection and socialization influences on behavioral congruence in adolescent peer groups provides rather compelling evidence for the claim that bonding to deviant groups is a major cause of delinquency and drug use. The evidence is indirect but substantial.

In sum, the available research evidence is generally consistent with the empirical claims of the integrated model. On some issues the evidence is very limited and on others it is equivocal, but to our knowledge, none of the empirical claims of this model can be rejected a priori on the basis of existing research evidence. We turn, therefore, to a test of this model with longitudinal data from a national probability sample of American youth.

NOTES

1. Pure control theorists make two claims concerning the relationship between bonding to delinquent peers and delinquency: That this relationship is spurious and explained by variation in conventional restraints; or that association with delinquent peers is an effect of delinquency rather than a cause (Hirschi, 1969; Hirschi and Gottfredson, 1980). The pattern of relationships discussed here clearly refutes the spuriousness claim insofar as it argues that this relationship is explained by variation in conventional restraints. The research cited in the remainder of this section further supports the independent predictive power of delinquent peer bonding measures. The second argument is of course a logical possibility whenever the analysis involves cross-sectional data because the causal direction is ambiguous. It is interesting however, that control theorists use this argument only with respect to the delinquent peer association-delinquency relationship when it obviously applies equally to the conventional bonding-delinquency relationship. In both cases, short of controlling for the temporal order of the measures in the analysis, the causal ordering is derived solely from theory and not from the data. It thus constitutes a very weak argument for accepting one theory as compared to another. In the test presented here, the temporal order of independent and dependent variables is controlled and the genuine predictive power of delinquent bonding measures is more clearly established. We also review several longitudinal studies relative to this issue in a subsequent section of this chapter.

2. The higher level of explained variance in the Linden study can be explained by the differences in the sample and the conventional bonding measures used. The fact

that a delinquency item (skipped school) is used as one of the predictors of delinquency could easily account for this difference.

3. The set actually included two measures: (1) number of friends using marijuana and (2) social support for marijuana use. This second measure confounded parent and peer support and contributed little to the total variance in marijuana use explained by the set. Virtually all of the explanatory power of this set can thus be attributed to the measure of number of friends using marijuana.

4. In most cases, the temporal ordering of predictor and criterion measures in cross-sectional studies on delinquency and drug use is the reverse of that specified in traditional causal models. Measures of current attachment to parents, current perceptions of limited opportunities, and current involvement with delinquent peers are used to explain delinquent and drug use that occurred in the past year or in one's entire lifetime. In many respects, the most plausible interpretation of these data are that strain, weak conventional bonds, and bonding to delinquent peers are all effects of one's involvement in delinquent behavior.

5. Total explained variance due to this subset of predictor clusters as well as the increases in explained variance due to parental influences and beliefs-values clusters were calculated from the data presented.

6. The theoretical model in this study postulated that strain led to an attenuation of one's commitment to conventional norms; weak bonding to conventional norms, when combined with commitment and attachment to delinquent peers, led to delinquent behavior. It is possible to argue that some of the strain measures, e.g., school achievement, commitment to parents, home success (perceived parental acceptance), reflect conventional bonding rather than strain, although that was not the conceptualization used in the study. The Community Success-Failure and School Status Deprivation Scales, on the other hand, were clearly strain measures and not conventional bonding measures. In this discussion these two measures are the ones referred to as strain measures. The others are treated as conventional bonding measures. Normlessness and Social Isolation scales were conceptualized as measures of commitment to conventional norms and perceived involvement with parents/school; i.e., as conventional bonding measures.

7. This claim is based upon beta weights from the final regression equation (see Table 7-6, Elliott and Voss, 1974: 184).

5

Description of the Study

GENERAL DESIGN

The National Youth Survey (NYS), a longitudinal study of delinquency and drug use among American youth, was designed to meet three primary objectives: (1) to provide a comprehensive description of the prevalence and incidence of delinquent behavior and drug use in the American youth population; (2) to examine the causal relationship between delinquent behavior and drug use; and (3) to test an integrated theoretical model of delinquent behavior. Our concern here is with this last objective.

The NYS involves a longitudinal, sequential design with multiple birth cohorts. The sample, selected in 1976, was a national probability sample of youths aged 11 to 17 and thus included seven birth cohorts (1959-1965). The total youth sample was initially interviewed between January and March of 1977 concerning their involvement in delinquent behavior and drug use during the calendar year 1976. The second and third surveys were conducted during this same period in successive years. By the third survey (1979), the panel was 13 through 19 years of age. The research reported in this volume is based on data from these three surveys, a period during which most panel members were adolescents.

THE SAMPLE

The National Youth Survey employed a probability sample of households in the continental United States in 1976 based upon a multistage, cluster sampling design. At each stage, the probabilities of selection were established to provide a self-weighting sample. Seventy-six primary sampling units were selected, with probability of selection being proportional to size. This sampling procedure resulted in the listing of 67,266 households of which approximately 8,000 were selected for inclusion in the sample. All youths living in the selected households who were 11 through 17 years of age on December 31, 1976, and were physically and mentally capable of being interviewed were eligible respondents for the study. The selected households generated an estimated 2,360 eligible youths. Of these, 635 (27 percent) did not participate in the study due to (1) parental refusal, (2) youth refusal, or (3) an inability to make contact with the respondent. The remaining 1,725 agreed to participate in the study, signed informed consents, and completed interviews in the initial (1977) survey. An age, sex, and race comparison between nonparticipating eligible youths and participating youths indicates that the loss rate from any particular age, sex, or racial group appears to be proportional to that group's representation in the population. Further, with respect to these characteristics, participating youth appear to be representative of the total 11- through 17-year-old youth population in the United States as established by the U.S. Census Bureau. For a detailed, technical description of the sample and the initial loss analysis see Huizinga (1978) and Elliott et al. (1981).

PANEL MORTALITY

Respondent loss over the first three surveys was relatively small. The loss rate for the 1978 survey was 4 percent (N = 70), and for the 1979 survey, the cumulative loss increased to 6 percent (N = 99). A comparison of participants and nonparticipants at the second and third waves revealed some selective loss by ethnicity, class, and place of residence. There did not appear to be any selective loss by sex or age, nor did it appear that there was any selective loss relative to self-reported levels of delinquent behavior. The few significant differences found indicated that those lost reported less delinquency on the first and second waves than those participating each year. Comparisons of participants across the first three waves indicated that the loss by age, sex, ethnicity, class, place of residence, and reported delinquency did not influence the underlying distributions on these variables in any substantial way. We thus conclude that the representativeness of the sample with respect to these variables has not been affected in any serious way by the loss over the first three surveys. For a detailed description of the loss analyses across the first three years, see Elliott et al. (1981).

GENERAL STRUCTURE OF
THE ANALYSES

The basic approach to testing the integrated theoretical model described in earlier chapters involves the use of a linear or structural equation model that incorporates measures of the major conceptual variables specified by the theory. The full multivariate complexity and temporal ordering of the theoretical constructs can be analyzed with this approach. Given the longitudinal design of the study and three annual waves of data for each subject, two independent tests of the model were undertaken, using one-year lagged predictor and criterion variables. The initial analysis thus involved data from the 1977 and 1978 surveys, and this analysis was independently replicated using data from the 1978 and 1979 surveys. Similar results from both analyses would strengthen the interpretation of findings.

MEASURES OF VARIABLES IN
THE THEORETICAL MODEL

Predictor measures. The use of the above analytical procedure requires the selection of a set of indicators for each of

<u>STRAIN</u>
  *Family Aspirations/Achievement Scale
  *School Aspirations/Achievement Scale
  Future Educational Goal/Expectation Discrepancy
  Future Occupational Goal/Expectation Discrepancy

<u>CONVENTIONAL BONDING</u>

A. External (Social)
  *Family Involvement Scale
  *School Scholastic Involvement Scale
  School Athletic Involvement Scale
  School Activities Involvement Scale
  Community Involvement Scale
  Family Labeling Scale
  Teacher Labeling Scale
  Perceived Sanctions in Family Scale

B. Internal (Personal)
  *Family Normlessness Scale
  *School Normlessness Scale
  Family Social Isolation Scale
  School Social Isolation Scale
  Family Aspirations Scale
  School Aspirations Scale
  Future Educational Goals
  Future Occupational Goals

<u>DEVIANT PEER BONDING</u>

A. External (Social)
  *Involvement with Deviant Peers Index
  Peer Sanctions - Involvement Index
  Peer Involvement Scale
  Exposure to Delinquent Peers
  Perceived Sanctions by Peers

B. Internal (Personal)
  *Attitudes Towards Deviance Scale
  Commitment to Delinquent Peers Scale
  Peer Normlessness
  Peer Social Isolation

* Selected measures for the causal modeling analysis

Figure 5.1: Outline of Theoretical Variables and Sets of Measures

the theoretical constructs in the model. Twenty-five specific measures of strain, conventional bonding, and deviant bonding were organized into variable sets as indicated in Figure 5.1. As our initial plan involved the use of the LISREL technique, at least two measures of each of the major theoretical variables were needed, but it was not practical to include all twenty-five predictors in the analysis, nor was this necessary to adequately evaluate the model or the predictive utility of this set of predictors. Based upon a sequence of correlation and stepwise regression analyses, a smaller set of predictor measures was selected for the causal modeling analysis.

The criteria for selection were (1) that each variable set be represented by at least one predictor; (2) that each relevant institutional context (i.e., family, school, and peers) be represented by at least one predictor; and (3) that the predictors selected from each set account for the majority of the explained variance attributable to that entire set of predictors. This process resulted in the selection of eight predictor measures: Two strain, four conventional bonding, and two deviant bonding measures (indicated by asterisks in Figure 5.1). Findings based upon this set of eight predictors should approximate the results that would have been obtained had the entire set of twenty-five predictors been used in the analysis. The selected predictor measures are described briefly below. The psychometric properties of each of the scales in the total set of measures are presented in Appendix A.

Strain. The strain measures reflect the discrepancy between a set of cultural expectations endorsed by the subject as important goals and his or her perceived realization of these goals. The two measures selected to represent the set of strain measures involve goal expectation discrepancies in the home and school contexts. Specifically, a three-point response set, "Very Important," "Somewhat Important," and "Not Important at All," was used to measure the respondent's endorsement of five family and school goals. In the family context the goals were: (1) getting along well with your parents; (2) having your parents think you do things well; (3) having a family that does a lot of things together; (4) having parents who comfort you when you are unhappy about something; and (5) having parents you can talk to about almost anything. The goals in the school context were: (1) having a high grade point average; (2) having others think of you as a good student; (3) doing your own work without help from others; (4) doing well even in hard subjects; and (5) having teachers think of you as a good student. Perceived success in achieving these goals was assessed by means of a second three-point response set, "Very Well," "OK," and "Not Well at All," that reflects how well the subject thought he or she was doing in each of these areas. A cross-classification of these two responses was scored from 1 ("Very Important," "Very Well") to 6 ("Very Important," "Not Well at All") for each item, and a scale score obtained by summing over the five items.[1] A high score on the strain measures reflects a high perceived discrepancy between personally endorsed goals and present achievement with respect to these goals in each of these social settings.

The two most common measures of strain, perceived chances of achieving future educational and occupational goals, were not used in this analysis. The home and school strain measures were stronger predictors of subsequent delinquent behavior and adequately account for the total explained variance of the entire set of strain predictors. They are probably more salient indicators of strain because they reflect personal frustrations located in the present as opposed to the future.

Conventional bonds. Four scales are used to assess bonding to the conventional social order. The Family and School Involvement scales assess the amount of time spent with the family and on academic concerns at school. These scales reflect involvement in conventional settings and activities. Each context-specific scale is composed of three items that ask respondents to report the number of afternoons and evenings in an average week, Monday through Friday, they spend in each setting, in addition to time spent in each setting on the weekends. The first two items on each scale had an open-ended response set (from zero to five afternoons or evenings) whereas the item on weekend involvement had a five-point Likert response set ranging from "A great deal" to "Very little." Scores on the three items are summed, with a high score reflecting a high level of involvement in that particular conventional setting or activity.

The Normlessness scales assess the subject's commitment to conventional social norms at home and at school. Conceptually, normlessness refers to the belief that one must violate the rules/norms to achieve personal goals or aspirations. This form of normative commitment is measured in both the family (four items) and school (five items) contexts. A five-point Likert response set ranging from "Strongly Agree" to "Strongly Disagree" is employed with this scale (see Appendix A for psychometric properties). The scale is scored such that a high score reflects a high commitment to the conventional norms in that context.

Bonding to delinquent peers. Integration into a delinquent peer group is measured by a joint consideration of the involvement or time spent with peers and the delinquent/conventional orientation of the peer group. The peer involvement measure assesses the amount of time spent with friends during afternoons, evenings, and weekends in an average week. It is scored the same as the family and school involvement measures previously described. The Exposure to Delinquent Peers scale measures the proportion of a subject's close friends who engage in each of ten different illegal acts. These acts range from trivial offenses (e.g., theft less than $5) to very serious, felony crimes. The five-point response set ranges from "All of them" to "None of them." The combined peer involvement/exposure to delinquent peers measure (labeled "Involvement with Delinquent Peers Index") is defined as the peer involvement (PI) score multiplied by the difference between the exposure to delinquent peers (EDP) score and the mean of the exposure scale; i.e., $PI \times (EDP - \overline{EDP})$. This Involvement with Delinquent Peers Index is large and positive for youths heavily involved with a delinquent peer group and negatively large for youths heavily involved with conventional peers. Hence, a high positive score implies strong bonding to a delinquent peer group.

The Attitudes Toward Deviance scale assesses the subject's personal beliefs about how wrong it is to commit certain deviant acts.[2] A four-point response set ranging from "Very wrong" to "Not wrong at all" is used with the items for this scale. A high score on this nine-item scale reflects a conventional, pro-social orientation toward behavior.

Measures of delinquency and drug use. A new self-reported measure of delinquent behavior was developed for the National Youth Survey, designed specifically to address the major critcisms of prior self-report measures (see Hindelang et al., 1975, 1981; Nettler, 1974; Farrington, 1973; Reiss, 1975; Elliott and Ageton, 1980). These criticisms focused upon the unrepresentativeness of items (usually trivial, nonserious offenses including some that were not technically violations of the law); normative response sets ("never," "once or twice," and "three or more times") that did not provide a precise frequency estimate and severely truncated the true frequency distributions; item overlap that produced multiple counting of single events; and extended reporting periods ("ever," "over the past three years") that generated serious problems for the accuracy of recall.

The self-report measure developed for the NYS included 47 items that were selected so as to be representative of the full range of official acts for which juveniles could be arrested. The set included all but one of the UCR Part I offenses (homicide was excluded); 60 percent of Part II offenses, and a wide range of UCR "other offenses." We also attempted to construct items with more precise descriptions of behavior so as to reduce or eliminate the potential for item overlap and multiple counting. Two response sets were used: An open-ended frequency count and a series of categories for all frequency responses of ten or higher. These response sets provide better discrimination at the high end of the frequency continuum and are more suited to estimating the actual number of offenses committed. For the purpose of this theory test, the categorical responses are used in all but one analysis because they have better distributional characteristics and are less skewed. The one use of the frequency response data is clearly indicated.

Compared with other self-reported delinquency measures, the NYS measure involves a moderate recall period (one year) and permits a direct comparison to other self-report and official measures that are reported for a calendar year. A more detailed review of the criticisms of earlier self-reported delinquency measures and the construction of NYS measure may be found in Elliott and Ageton (1980) and Elliott et al. (1983). In addition to the self-reported delinquency items, the NYS included 15 questions about drug use. The items covered all common drug substances (i.e., alcohol, tobacco, marijuana, amphetamines, barbiturates, and tranquilizers) as well as a fairly comprehensive set of less common drugs (i.e., hallucinogens, heroin, cocaine, PCP, and inhalants). The response set for the drug items was identical to the categorical set used for the self-reported delinquency questions.

To test the adequacy of the theoretical model for different types of delinquency and drug use, several delinquency and drug use scales have been constructed as criterion variables. Our use of specific scales was guided by a desire to test the model's explanatory power for general or common delinquency and drug use, as well as its ability to account for serious and minor involvement in these behaviors. The following scales were used as measures of delinquency: (1) General Delinquency—a summary measure of all the delinquency items except some of the more trivial items (such as lied about age, hitchhiked illegally, and bought liquor for a minor); (2) Index Offenses—a scale including all Part I index offenses (except homicide and arson); and (3) Minor Delinquency—a seven-item scale containing a range of minor illegal acts such as joyriding, being a runaway, disorderly conduct, and theft of less than $5. As drug use measures, we used the single item measuring marijuana use and a Drug Use scale that includes the use of different illicit drugs. Figure 5.2 presents these scales and the specific items contained in each.

Temporal order. The test of the theoretical model includes eight predictor variables reflecting strain at home and school, bonding to the family and school, and bonding to deviant peers. Five specific measures of delinquency and drug use are used as criterion variables. Figure 5.3 portrays the time location of these measures. As may be seen from Figure 5.3, some of the variables provide point estimates (i.e., those that reflect attitudes or aspirations at the time of the interview) and others provide interval estimates (i.e., cover the period of the calender year prior to the interview). The time location of the measures is important because a causal interpretation is strengthened when the temporal order is controlled in the analysis. Given both point and interval estimates, we could not always insure this temporal ordering on an annual basis without a very long time lag (i.e., two years). For example, using only interval

Drug Use
1) Hallucinogens
2) Amphetamines
3) Barbiturates
4) Heroin
5) Cocaine

Minor Delinquency
1) Hit teacher
2) Hit parent
3) Theft LT$5
4) Joyriding
5) Disorderly conduct
6) Panhandled
7) Runaway

Index Offenses
1) Aggravated assault
2) Sexual assault
3) Gang fights
4) Stole motor vehicle
5) Stole something GT$50
6) Broke into bldg./vehicle
7) Strongarmed students
8) Strongarmed teachers
9) Strongarmed others

General Delinquency
1) Stole motor vehicle
2) Stole something GT$50
3) Bought stolen goods
4) Runaway
5) Carried hidden weapon
6) Stole something LT$5
7) Aggravated assault
8) Prostitution
9) Sexual intercourse
10) Gang fights
11) Sold marijuana
12) Hit teacher
13) Hit parent
14) Hit students
15) Disorderly conduct
16) Sold hard drugs
17) Joyriding
18) Sexual assault
19) Strongarmed students
20) Strongarmed teachers
21) Strongarmed others
22) Stole something $5-50
23) Broke into bldg./vehicle
24) Panhandled

Figure 5.2: Specific Delinquency and Drug Use Scales

estimates, Family and School Involvement 1 (see Figure 5.3) would be used to predict Involvement with Delinquent Peers 2, which would be used to predict Self-Reported Delinquency 3. In this case the measure of the dependent variable (delinquent behavior) occurs two years after that of the initial predictor measure. We felt this was an unreasonable time lag and opted for a shorter one (one year) by controlling temporal sequences so that predictor measures are either temporally prior to or simultaneous with the criterion measure. Because the delinquency measures are interval estimates, we used interval predictor measures that were concurrent with delinquency/

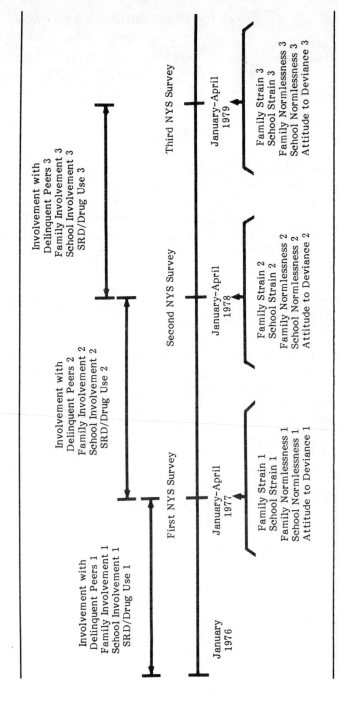

Figure 5.3: Time Location of the Measures

drug use measures; i.e., covered the same time period. Point predictor measures were always temporally prior to the criterion measures.[3]

SUMMARY

The test of the theoretical model presented here is based upon a national probability sample of American adolescents who were interviewed annually over three consecutive years (1977-1979). Eight predictor variables were selected from a larger set of predictors to be included in a causal modeling analysis. Five different measures of self-reported delinquent behavior and drug use were employed as criterion measures. The temporal ordering of the variables was controlled in the analysis, with all predictor variables being temporally antecedent or concurrent with the measures of delinquency and drug use. The analysis plan involved an initial test of the model's power to explain delinquency and drug use during 1977 using predictors obtained prior to and during this same year and a replication of this analysis using predictors obtained in 1977 and 1978 to explain delinquency and drug use during 1978. We turn now to an initial multivariate test of the integrated theoretical model.

NOTES

1. Scoring was based upon the following scheme:

How well are you doing?

		Very Well	OK	Not Well
How Important?	Very	1	4	6
	Somewhat	2	3	5
	Not at All	3	3	3

2. There is some ambiguity about the conceptualization of this measure. On the one hand, it could be treated as a measure of internal conventional bonding—belief in the moral validity of the norms. In addition it has been used in prior studies as a measure of commitment to delinquent norms, reflecting socialization processes within delinquent groups. For tests of differential association it has been treated as the critical intervening variable between association with delinquent peers and delinquent behavior. We reject this latter view, and have conceptualized it here as one dimension of internal bonding to a delinquent peer group. But we acknowledge that it also could be viewed as a measure of commitment to conventional norms derived from early socialization experiences in the family and school. We thus treated it as an independent predictor variable in the analysis to facilitate its interpretation.

3. There is one exception to this general rule. The Attitudes Towards Deviance measure was conceptualized as an internal bonding to delinquent peers measure, an intervening variable in the theoretical model. Because strain and conventional bonding measures are assumed to be temporally prior to this measure, we used the Time 2 measure of this scale as the predictor measure in the initial test of the model and the Time 3 measure as the predictor in the replication as presented here. We also examined Time 1 and Time 2 measures of this scale in tests of the model. The effect of using the Time 2 and 3 measures rather than Time 1 and 2 measures is minimal.

6

An Initial Multivariate Test of the Integrated Theory

ANALYSIS DESIGN

To examine the empirical relationships among the variables described in the earlier theoretical model, a linear or structural equation model approach was used. This approach allows examination of the full miltivariate nature of the theoretical model, determines the relative importance of each of the variables, and provides an examination of whether the empirical relationships among the variables are consistent with various causal propositions of the theory. Initially it was anticipated that the coefficients of the structural equations specifying the relationships between theoretical variables would be estimated by the LISREL program (Joreskog and Sorbom, 1978). However, because of various procedural difficulties in applying the LISREL approach,[1] standard path analyses were used. The use of path analysis requires some caution because the potential problems associated with measurement error may not be handled by standard regression techniques (see Cook and Campbell, 1979). It should also be noted that the hypothesized interaction between conventional and deviant bonding is not addressed here, but will be considered in detail in Chapter 7.

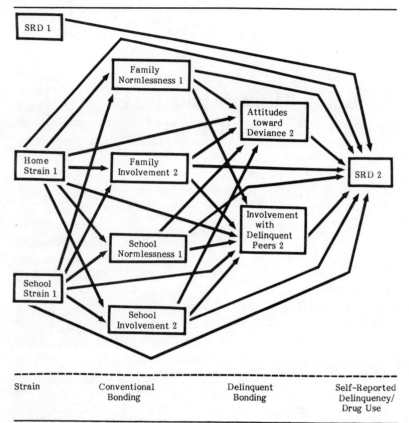

Figure 6.1: The Full Path Model

The full path model specified by the theory and the variables selected to represent the various theoretical constructs are presented in Figure 6.1. As can be seen in the figure, strain leads to changes in conventional bonding, delinquent bonding, and delinquent behavior/drug use; changes in conventional bonding lead to changes in the level of bonding with delinquent peers and changes in delinquent/behavior and drug use; and changes in bonding to delinquent peers leads to changes in delinquency and drug use involvement. Prior self-reported delinquency or drug use is included as an exogenous variable in the model, affecting the predicted involvement in delinquency or drug use. Thus, the effect of changes in theoretical constructs on future delinquency or drug use is determined in conjunction with the effect of prior delinquency or drug use.

Because the National Youth Survey provides longitudinal data, the time ordering of the variables can be arranged so that it is consonant with the causal ordering of the integrated theory. In all cases, a variable that is assumed to have a causal effect on another is measured prior to or concurrently with the criterion variable. As noted earlier, some of the variables are measures of behavior over the calender year whereas others are point estimates of attitudes at the time of the interview. The former include self-reported delinquency and drug use, and involvement in family, school, and peer activities. The latter includes strain, normlessness, and attitude toward deviance measures.

The exact time ordering of the variables representing events occurring throughout the calender year cannot be precisely determined. Conceivably, all reported behaviors of a particular kind could have occurred in a given month or week at the beginning of the year whereas all reported behaviors of another kind occurred at the end of the year. This spacing of events is considered to be highly unlikely, and it is assumed that these interval or calender year measures reflect behaviors occurring more evenly throughout the year.

Given the three interview periods under study, it would be possible to have all predictor variables temporally precede the criterion variables. Such an arrangement, however, would require a two-year lag between the change in one variable and the related change in another (e.g., strain and delinquency). This time interval was considered too long for the kinds of effects postulated by the integrated model. As a result, the path model spans only a two-year period and certain cause and effect dyads involve variables measured concurrently. The use of the concurrent measures is not necessarily inappropriate, however, because certain relationships may be expected to operate at more or less the same time. For example, involvement in pro-social activities may be anticipated to reduce involvement with delinquent peers on a simple availability of time basis. In the full path model presented in Figure 6.1, the two-year time interval is indicated by variables measured in the first year labeled by a 1 and those measured in the second year by a 2.

To examine the relationships described by the theory, path coefficients and their standard errors were obtained for the full model for different kinds of delinquent behavior and drug use. Separate analyses were conducted for the General Delinquency scale, the UCR Part I or Index scale, the Minor Delinquency scale, marijuana use, and the Illicit Drug Use scale. To examine potential sex differences, the analyses were performed for the total NYS sample and separately for males and females.

For each of these full models, nonsignificant paths were deleted, producing a reduced or simplified model, and the path coefficients were recalculated for the reduced model. Statistical computations were performed by a modified version of an interactive path analysis program described by Nygreen (1971). The determination of which paths were nonsignificant was based both on standard statistical tests of the regression coefficients and on the percentage of variance explained by individual or groups of variables. The use of both requirements is beneficial not only on practical grounds (statistical significance, being dependent on sample size, may indicate significance of variables that have only trivial effects on other variables) but also because measurement errors are most likely not independently normally distributed, especially for the delinquency and drug use measures. These distributional assumptions are needed for the application of the standard statistical tests.

Because the estimation procedure used in determining the path coefficients will take advantage of the unique features of the particular data used, the above analyses were independently replicated. The first analyses were performed using 1976 and 1977 data, and the second or replication analyses were performed using the same variables from the 1977 and 1978 data. Dissimilar results from these replications would make the findings of the path analyses questionable.

Given the above, the general analysis strategy can be described as two replications of a sequence of path analyses.

Separate path analyses are performed for the total sample, for males, and for females using each of five delinquency or drug use measures (a general offense measure and measures of index offenses, minor offenses, marijuana use, and illicit drug use). For each analysis, a reduced or simplified path model is obtained.

RESULTS FROM PATH ANALYSES

The path coefficients, standard errors, residual paths, and multiple correlation ratios for the full path model with the General Delinquency scale (SRD) as the final criterion variable are presented in Table 6.1. The data upon which this analysis is based are the 1976 and 1977 NYS data for the total sample. Examination of the path coefficients and standard errors suggests that a simplified model could be constructed. Deleting the nonsignificant paths (i.e., those paths for which a test of the hypothesis that the path coefficient is zero cannot be rejected at the .01 level or which are only barely significant) produces the reduced model pictured in Figure 6.2. As seen in this figure, the only direct paths leading to self-reported delinquency are from the Involvement with Delinquent Peers Index and prior SRD measure. The strain variables affect the conventional bonding variables that, in turn, affect involvement with delinquent peers, but neither strain nor conventional bonding variables have a direct influence on delinquency.

Reduced models identical to that pictured in Figure 6.2 were obtained for both males and females, for all delinquent and drug use behaviors considered, across both replications of the set of path analyses. The adequacy of the reduced model in capturing the variances of the full model can be seen in Table 6.2, which lists the correlation ratio for each endogenous variable in the full and reduced models. As seen in the table, the vast majority of the endogenous variables lose less than 1 percent of explained variance in moving from the full to the reduced model, a few lose 2 percent, and three lose 3 percent. Because of the consistent adequacy[2] of the reduced model and the underlying similarity of the path analyses of the full model

TABLE 6.1
Path Coefficients, Standard Errors, Residual Paths, and Multiple Correlation Ratios for the Full Path Model with General Delinquency as the Criterion Variable

Path Analysis

Path Coefficients and Standard Errors

P(4,2) =	-.2896	(+/- .030)
P(4,3) =	-.0435	(+/- .029)
P(5,2) =	-.2500	(+/- .030)
P(5,3) =	.0421	(+/- .029)
P(6,2) =	-.2175	(+/- .029)
P(6,3) =	-.1492	(+/- .029)
P(7,2) =	-.1331	(+/- .029)
P(7,3) =	-.1042	(+/- .029)
P(8,2) =	.0208	(+/- .030)
P(8,3) =	.0509	(+/- .029)
P(8,4) =	-.0947	(+/- .036)
P(8,5) =	-.1461	(+/- .029)
P(8,6) =	-.2247	(+/- .036)
P(8,7) =	-.1874	(+/- .029)
P(9,2) =	.0585	(+/- .030)
P(9,3) =	-.0116	(+/- .029)
P(9,4) =	-.1840	(+/- .036)
P(9,5) =	-.1710	(+/- .029)
P(9,6) =	-.1764	(+/- .036)
P(9,7) =	-.1414	(+/- .029)
P(10,1) =	-.3706	(+/- .030)
P(10,2) =	-.0225	(+/- .026)
P(10,3) =	.0178	(+/- .025)
P(10,4) =	.0133	(+/- .032)
P(10,5) =	-.0176	(+/- .026)
P(10,6) =	.0487	(+/- .032)
P(10,7) =	.0052	(+/- .026)
P(10,8) =	.4832	(+/- .036)
P(10,9) =	.0268	(+/- .031)

Variable List:

Variable No.   Variable Name (Time period indicated by a 1 or 2)

No.	Variable Name
1	General Delinquency - 1
2	Family Strain - 1
3	School Strain - 1
4	Family Normlessness - 1
5	Family Involvement - 2
6	School Normlessness - 1
7	School Involvement - 2
8	Involvement with Delinquent Peers - 2
9	Attitudes toward Deviance - 1
10	General Delinquency - 2

Residual Paths and R-Squared

P(4,A) =	.9522	(.09)
P(5,B) =	.9706	(.06)
P(6,C) =	.9544	(.09)
P(7,D) =	.9814	(.04)
P(8,E) =	.8855	(.22)
P(9,F) =	.8772	(.23)
P(10,G) =	.6876	(.53)

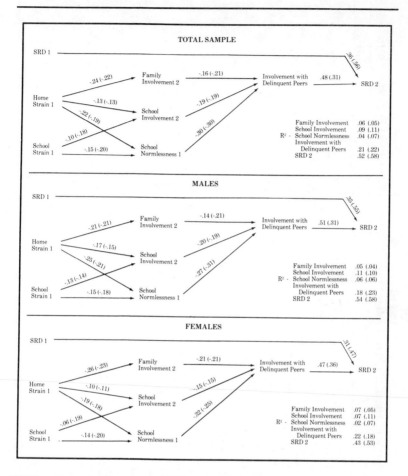

NOTE: General delinquency (SRD) path coefficients and correlation ratios of replication analyses (1977 to 1978) are enclosed in parentheses.

Figure 6.2: Reduced Path Model: General Delinquency

for different sexes, behaviors, and replications, the tables listing the full path analysis results have been relegated to Appendix B.[3]

The path coefficients and the correlation ratios of the endogenous variables of the reduced path model for general delinquency are shown in Figure 6.2. This figure summarizes the path analyses for the total sample and for males and females

TABLE 6.2
Multiple Correlation Ratios (correlations of replication study, 1977 to 1978, enclosed in parentheses)

	Total Sample		Males		Females	
	Full	Reduced	Full	Reduced	Full	Reduced
General Delinquency	.53 (.59)	.52 (.58)	.55 (.58)	.54 (.58)	.44 (.54)	.43 (.53)
Index	.32 (.36)	.32 (.36)	.38 (.37)	.37 (.36)	.13 (.21)	.11 (.21)
Minor	.40 (.45)	.39 (.44)	.42 (.46)	.41 (.45)	.34 (.41)	.33 (.40)
Marijuana	.61 (.60)	.59 (.59)	.64 (.63)	.62 (.62)	.57 (.54)	.55 (.51)
Hard Drugs	.34 (.30)	.34 (.29)	.51 (.36)	.50 (.34)	.15 (.19)	.14 (.18)
Family Normlessness	.09 (.14)	– –	.12 (.14)	– –	.07 (.14)	– –
Family Involvement	.06 (.05)	.06 (.05)	.05 (.05)	.05 (.04)	.07 (.05)	.07 (.05)
School Normlessness	.09 (.11)	.09 (.11)	.11 (.10)	.11 (.10)	.07 (.11)	.07 (.11)
School Involvement	.04 (.07)	.04 (.07)	.06 (.06)	.06 (.06)	.02 (.07)	.02 (.07)
Involvement with Delinquent Peers	.22 (.24)	.21 (.22)	.19 (.26)	.18 (.23)	.23 (.21)	.22 (.18)
Attitudes toward Deviance	.23 (.28)	– –	.22 (.28)	– –	.22 (.25)	– –

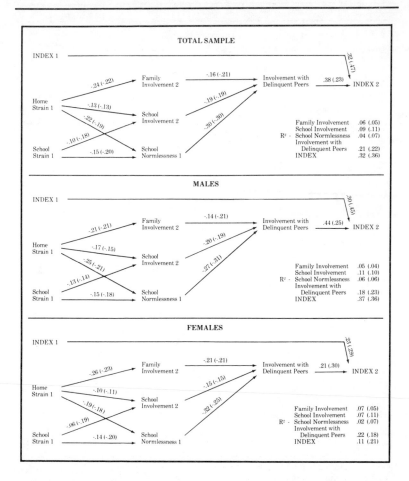

NOTE: Path coefficients and correlation ratios of replication analyses (1977 to 1978) are enclosed in parentheses.

Figure 6.3: Reduced Path Model: Index Offenses (INDEX)

across both replications. Similar summaries of the path analyses of the reduced model for index offenses, minor offenses, marijuana use, and illicit drug use are contained in Figures 6.3 through 6.6, respectively. It should be noted that the analyses for the strain, bonding, and involvement with delinquent peer variables are all identical and only the coefficients of the paths

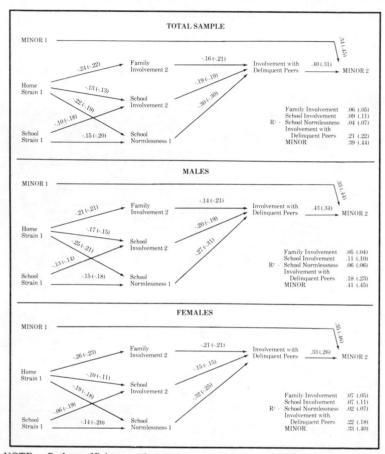

NOTE: Path coefficients and correlation ratios of replication analyses (1977 to 1978) are enclosed in parentheses.

Figure 6.4: Reduced Path Model: Minor Offenses (MINOR)

leading to the different forms of delinquent behavior are altered in these analyses.

As can be seen in Figures 6.2 to 6.6, the relationships among the social-psychological variables are similar to those that would be expected on the basis of the earlier theoretical development. For both males and females and the total sample, increases in strain at home lead to decreases in family involve-

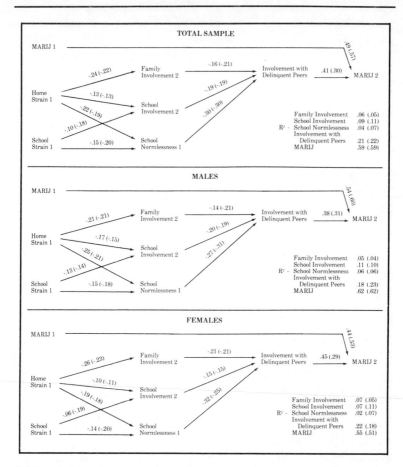

NOTE: Path coefficients and correlation ratios of replication analyses (1977 to 1978) are enclosed in parentheses.

Figure 6.5: Reduced Path Model: Marijuana Use (MARIJ)

ment, school involvement, and school normlessness (recall that normlessness is reverse scored, so that a reduced score implies increasing alienation). Similarly, increases in school strain lead to decreases in school involvement and school normlessness. Increases in the conventional bonding measures (i.e., family involvement, school involvement, school normlessness) lead to decreases in involvement with delinquent peers.

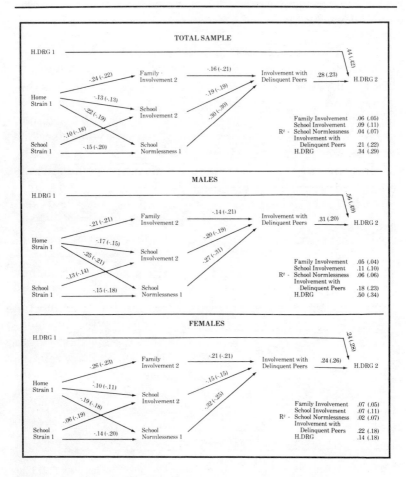

NOTE: Path coefficients and correlation ratios of replication analyses (1977 to 1978) are enclosed in parentheses.

Figure 6.6: Reduced Path Model: Hard Drug Use (H.DRG)

The strain variables do not, however, have a direct effect on involvement with delinquent peers. The magnitude of the relationships are generally consistent across sexes and replications, but all are relatively small. Examination of the R^2 values for the endogenous social-psychological variables indicates that the variables included in the analyses do a relatively poor job of predicting these social-psychological variables.

As noted earlier, this low predictablility does not result from the construciton of the reduced model from the full model (see Table 6.2). Increases in the ability to explain changes in the levels of these variables thus lies in variables not included in the initial variables set selection. The issue of including other variables as measures of strain or conventional bonding, or of other theoretical constructs such as neighborhood social disorganization to increase the level of explanation raises the potential problem of specification error. Conceivably, the addition of other relevant variables to the model could alter the computed path coefficients (see, for example, Cook and Campbell, 1979). Given the consistency of the path analyses, however, it would seem that although the magnitude of the coefficients might change, it is unlikely that the basic relationships would.

The only variables having a direct effect on the delinquency and drug use measures are involvement with delinquent peers and prior delinquency or drug use. Neither the strain nor the conventional bonding measures have a direct effect on delinquency or drug use. Although this pattern is consistent across sexes and replications, it should be observed that the relative importance of involvement with delinquent peers and prior delinquency in predicting delinquency is often reversed in the two replications. This reversal can be observed for both males and females on the general delinquency measure, and for males on the index and minor offense measures. Prior drug use appears to be a somewhat better predictor of future drug use than involvement with delinquent peers for boys. For girls the influence of the two predictors is approximately equal, except for the second replication for marijuana use. There, prior marijuana use can be seen to have a greater effect on future marijuana use.

Examination of the R^2 values for the delinquency and drug use measures indicates a lower overall level of prediction for females, especially for index offenses and illicit drug use. For both males and females, prediction of overall involvement in delinquent behaviors and of marijuana use is higher than for index offenses, minor offenses, or illicit drug use, with more than 50 percent of the variance of general delinquency and marijuana use being explained in most instances. The ability to explain changes in index offenses, minor offenses, or illicit drug use is in general moderate for males (30-50 percent of the variance explained) and moderate to low for females (11-34 percent of the variance explained).

SUMMARY

As an overview of the results of the path analyses across sexes and replications, it appears that prior delinquency and involvement in delinquent peer groups are the main factors directly influencing both delinquency and drug use, and that in many cases the two predictor variables provide a reasonably good estimation of the level of involvement in delinquency and drug use. The social-psychological constructs of strain and conventional bonding, however, have only weak and indirect effects on delinquent behavior and drug use. Although strain leads to changes in conventional bonding and the level of conventional bonding affects the level of involvement with delinquent peers, these effects are relatively small.

NOTES

1. In the attempt to employ the LISREL technique to obtain estimates of the parameters of the structural equations defined by the theory, several different models or parameter specifications were tried. In all cases, either the iterative minimization procedure used in obtaining maximum likelihood estimates would not converge and successive estimates were becoming more and more unreasonable or the converged solutions were nonsensical, providing negative estimates of variances and inconsistent estimates of certain relationships. It is suspected that the LISREL approach that assumes a multivariate normal distribution may not be robust in the face of extreme nonnormality. Thus, the distributions of the various delinquency scales that have a mode of zero and are highly skewed may have led to the difficulties in using the LISREL method.

2. It should be noted that the large sample likelihood ratio test of the adequacy of the reduced models indicates that for certain models the fit of the reduced model to each dependent variable is as good as in the full model. For some models, however, the equivalence of the full and reduced models would be rejected at the .05 level. This test is relatively sensitive to sample size, however, and because the NYS sample is relatively large and the calculated Chi-Square values were relatively small in all cases, it was concluded that the fit of the reduced models was adequate.

3. The reduced path model tables are available from the authors upon request.

7

Examination of the
Conditional Relationship
Between Conventional
and Delinquent Bonding

The preceding path analyses indicated that only two variables, involvement with delinquent peers and prior delinquency, had direct effects on the level of involvement in delinquent behavior. The general path model did not, however, include the conditional relationship specified in the theoretical model. In the discussion of the theoretical model we postulated that the effect of involvement with delinquent peers on delinquent behavior varied by the level of bonding to conventional groups and activities. This chapter examines the question of whether there is an interaction between involvement with delinquent peers and level of conventional bonding in predicting delinquent behavior.

Using the same measures of conventional bonding, bonding to delinquent peers, and delinquency/drug use, it was anticipated that a linear model approach would be used in examining the potential interaction. However, the use of these methods (regression models, analyses of variance, analyses of covariance) was problematic because of unequal residual variances for different levels of bonding or because of the artificial restriction of range of the delinquency measures and the restulting hetroscedasticity of these measures for groups defined by different levels of conventional bonding. As a result, the interaction between involvement

with delinquent peers and bonding levels in relationship to delinquency is examined by comparing the delinquent behavior of
different groups of youths characterized by different levels of
conventional bonding and different levels of involvement with
delinquent peers. As in the previous analyses, two replications of
the same basic analysis can be made with the three years of data
available.

Although the assumptions required for linear model techniques
were violated and results from these models could not be unequiv-
ocally interpreted, it should be noted that the results from these
analyses were consistent with the existence of an interaction
between levels of conventional bonding and levels of bonding with
delinquent peers. For example, dividing the sample into groups
with lower and higher conventional bonds, the correlation between
the General Delinquency scale (SRD) and involvement with
delinquent peers was .42 for the group with high bonds and .65 for
the group with low bonds (initial test). Similarly, using both prior
delinquency and involvement with delinquent peers to predict
current delinquency, the multiple correlation ratio was .31 for the
high bonds group and .57 for the group with low bonds. Because
the comparable R^2 for the total sample was .52, the level of conventional bonding does appear to specify the relationship between
bonding to delinquent peers and delinquent behavior. And finally,
a standard multiple regression analysis was completed with the
sample in which the four interaction terms (conventional bonding
measures $\times$ involvement with delinquent peers) were included in
the regression along with the set of predictors used in the full path
analyses. The addition of the interaction terms resulted in a small
(two percent) but significant increase in explained variance (SRD2).

DETERMINATION OF TYPES OF YOUTHS
CHARACTERIZED BY DIFFERENT LEVELS OF
CONVENTIONAL BONDING AND INVOLVEMENT
WITH DELINQUENT PEERS

Given the multivariate measurement of the conventional
bonding domain, a K-means or iterative relocation cluster

analysis of the entire NYS sample was performed to locate types of youths with different patterns of conventional bonding characteristics.[1] Using the four measures of conventional bonding corresponding to the first two years of data, the clustering algorithm terminated on a two-cluster partition of the NYS sample. The first group was characterized by having, in general, lower than average scores. The group centroid was approximately one-half standard deviation below the mean on each of the conventional bonding variables. The second group was characterized by having higher than average scores, the group centroid being approximately one-half standard deviation above the mean on each conventional bonding variable. Although these groups are not distinct types, the analysis provides a minimum variance solution that divides the NYS sample into two groups, those with stronger than average bonds to conventional groups and activities and those with weaker than average bonds to these groups and activities. This cluster definition is used to identify youths with strong and weak conventional bonds. A replication of the cluster analysis using the bonding measures of the second and third years provided very similar results. Means and standard deviations of the conventional bonding variables for each cluster are compared with population values in Table 7.1.

To separate youths with higher and lower levels of involvement with delinquent peers a frequency distribution of the Involvement With Delinquent Peers Index was obtained. The median value was used to divide the sample into two groups, with the group below the median considered to have a low involvement and the group above the median a high involvement. The medians for the total NYS sample, for males and for females, were used as appropriate.

A cross-classification of individuals by conventional bonding level and level of involvement with delinquent peers thus produces four groups: Group 1, high conventional bonds and low involvement with delinquent peers; Group 2, high conventional bonds and high involvement with delinquent peers; Group 3, low conventional bonds and low involvement with delinquent peers; and Group 4, low conventional bonds and high involvement with delinquent peers.

TABLE 7.1
Mean Scores and Standard Deviations of the Conventional Bonding Measures for the Two Cluster Solutions

			Family Activities	Family Normlessness	School Activities	School Normlessness
1976-1977	Cluster 1 High Bonds N = 912	Mean S.D.	11.59 2.87	16.61 1.86	8.02 2.95	20.35 2.20
	Cluster 2 Low Bonds N = 699	Mean S.D.	8.06 3.41	13.19 2.05	5.55 3.07	16.79 2.27
	Total Sample N = 1611	Mean S.D.	10.06 3.57	15.13 2.58	6.95 3.24	18.81 2.85
1977-1978	Cluster 1 High Bonds N = 770	Mean S.D.	11.25 3.23	16.90 1.84	8.50 2.99	20.74 2.18
	Cluster 2 Low Bonds N = 725	Mean S.D.	8.23 3.51	13.75 2.05	5.28 3.18	17.14 2.37
	Total Sample N = 1495	Mean S.D.	9.78 3.69	15.37 2.50	6.94 3.48	18.99 2.90

SELF-REPORTED DELINQUENCY SCORES

To examine the effect of levels of conventional bonding and involvement with delinquent peers on delinquent behavior, it is necessary to adjust the measure of delinquent behavior for prior delinquency. Because prior delinquency predicts future delinquency, if conventional or deviant bonding levels are related to prior delinquency, differences in current delinquency between groups with differing bonding levels (conventional and deviant) may simply result from differences in prior delinquency.

To adjust the SRD2 scores, a linear regression equation with SRD2 as the dependent variable and SRD1 as the independent variable was obtained. For each respondent a new or adjusted SRD2 measure was obtained by subtracting the score predicted by the regression equation from the reported SRD2 score. In equation form, this is:

$$SRD2A = SRD2 - (b \, SRD1 + c)$$

where SRD2A is the adjusted score and b and c are the regression coefficient and constant. Thus, that part of the SRD2 score that can be linearly predicted by SRD1 has been removed, and the adjusted SRD2A score reflects the residual score from the regression line for that individual. It should be observed that the adjusted score can be either positive or negative because the adjusted score may reflect either an increase or decrease in delinquency from the level of the SRD2 score that would be predicted from the SRD1 score.

The above procedure was followed for each of the five delinquency and drug use scales used in this report. Separate regression lines and adjusted scores were obtained for each scale and for the total NYS sample, for males, and for females.

ANALYSIS RESULTS

The mean scores of the adjusted General Delinquency scale, the adjusted Index and Minor Offense scales, and the adjusted marijuana and illicit drug use measures for the total sample and for males and females were computed for the four groups defined by levels of conventional bonding and involvement with delinquent peers. These means were obtained for the 1976-1977 and the 1977-1978 periods and are presented in Tables 7.2 to 7.7. The statistical difference between the means was examined by unequal variance t-tests. As noted earlier, this multiple test approach was required because of the unequal variances and unequal sample sizes that precluded use of analysis of variance techniques.

Examination of Tables 7.2 to 7.7 reveals a relatively strong consistency in group differences across sexes for both delinquency and drug use measures. The two groups with low involvement with delinquent peers (i.e., those with either high or low levels of conventional bonding) are never statistically different on any delinquency or drug use measure for either sex or replication. These two groups have the lowest levels of involvement in delinquency and drug use. For both sexes, the group with high delinquent peer involvement and high conven-

(text continues on page 130)

TABLE 7.2
Means of Adjusted Delinquency and Drug Use Category Scale Scores
for Groups Defined by Levels of Conventional Bonding and Involvement
with Delinquent Peers: 1976 to 1977 for Total NYS Sample

			Delinquent Peer Involvement		Significance of Group Differences*			
	Conventional		Low	High	Group	Sig.	Group	Sig.
General	Bonding	High	-.94	.34	1,2	.00	2,3	.00
Delinquency		Low	-1.20	1.74	1,3	.28	2,4	.00
					1,4	.00	3,4	.00

			Delinquent Peer Involvement		Significance of Group Differences*			
	Conventional		Low	High	Group	Sig.	Group	Sig.
Index	Bonding	High	-.12	-.02	1,2	.08	2,3	.02
Offenses		Low	-.21	.31	1,3	.13	2,4	.00
					1,4	.00	3,4	.00

			Delinquent Peer Involvement		Significance of Group Differences*			
	Conventional		Low	High	Group	Sig.	Group	Sig.
Minor	Bonding	High	-.42	.20	1,2	.00	2,3	.00
Delinquency		Low	-.41	.63	1,3	.93	2,4	.00
					1,4	.00	3,4	.00

			Delinquent Peer Involvement		Significance of Group Differences*			
	Conventional		Low	High	Group	Sig.	Group	Sig.
Marijuana	Bonding	High	-.44	.08	1,2	.00	2,3	.00
Use		Low	-.43	.73	1,3	.82	2,4	.00
					1,4	.00	3,4	.00

			Delinquent Peer Involvement		Significance of Group Differences*			
	Conventional		Low	High	Group	Sig.	Group	Sig.
Illicit	Bonding	High	-.13	-.12	1,2	.82	2,3	.58
Drug Use		Low	-.07	.30	1,3	.47	2,4	.00
					1,4	.00	3,4	.00

* Significance - As determined by unequal variance t-test. Groups identified by the following scheme.

		Delinquent Peer Involvement		Group Sizes
	Conventional	Low	High	1 - 506
	Bonding High	Grp 1	Grp 2	2 - 281
	Low	Grp 3	Grp 4	3 - 192
				4 - 401

TABLE 7.3
Means of Adjusted Delinquency and Drug Use Category Scale Scores for Groups Defined by Levels of Conventional Bonding and Involvement with Delinquent Peers: 1976 to 1977, Males

| | | | Delinquent Peer Involvement | | Significance of Group Differences* | | | |
	Conventional		Low	High	Group	Sig.	Group	Sig.
General	Bonding	High	-1.35	1.10	1,2	.00	2,3	.00
Delinquency		Low	-1.90	2.26	1,3	.16	2,4	.12
					1,4	.00	3,4	.00

| | | | Delinquent Peer Involvement | | Significance of Group Differences* | | | |
	Conventional		Low	High	Group	Sig.	Group	Sig.
Index	Bonding	High	-.22	.18	1,2	.00	2,3	.00
Offenses		Low	-.35	.43	1,3	.36	2,4	.19
					1,4	.00	3,4	.00

| | | | Delinquent Peer Involvement | | Significance of Group Differences* | | | |
	Conventional		Low	High	Group	Sig.	Group	Sig.
Minor	Bonding	High	-.53	.42	1,2	.00	2,3	.00
Delinquency		Low	-.71	.80	1,3	.19	2,4	.16
					1,4	.00	3,4	.00

| | | | Delinquent Peer Involvement | | Significance of Group Differences* | | | |
	Conventional		Low	High	Group	Sig.	Group	Sig.
Marijuana	Bonding	High	-.52	.23	1,2	.00	2,3	.00
Use		Low	-.48	.73	1,3	.73	2,4	.02
					1,4	.00	3,4	.00

| | | | Delinquent Peer Involvement | | Significance of Group Differences* | | | |
	Conventional		Low	High	Group	Sig.	Group	Sig.
Illicit	Bonding	High	-.19	.01	1,2	.00	2,3	.01
Drug Use		Low	-.14	.28	1,3	.21	2,4	.02
					1,4	.00	3,4	.00

* Significance – As determined by unequal variance t-test. Groups identified by the following scheme.

| | | Delinquent Peer Involvement | | Group Sizes |
	Conventional	Low	High	
	Bonding High	Grp 1	Grp 2	1 – 255
	Low	Grp 3	Grp 4	2 – 113
				3 – 118
				4 – 228

TABLE 7.4

Means of Adjusted Delinquency and Drug Use Category Scale Scores for Groups Defined by Levels of Conventional Bonding and Involvement with Delinquent Peers: 1976 to 1977, Females

			Delinquent Peer Involvement		Significance of Group Differences*			
	Conventional		Low	High	Group	Sig.	Group	Sig.
General	Bonding	High	-.58	-.04	1,2	.02	2,3	.19
Delinquency		Low	-.46	1.14	1,3	.61	2,4	.00
					1,4	.00	3,4	.00

			Delinquent Peer Involvement		Significance of Group Differences*			
	Conventional		Low	High	Group	Sig.	Group	Sig.
Index	Bonding	High	-.03	-.09	1,2	.07	2,3	.15
Offenses		Low	-.01	.15	1,3	.64	2,4	.00
					1,4	.02	3,4	.09

			Delinquent Peer Involvement		Significance of Group Differences*			
	Conventional		Low	High	Group	Sig.	Group	Sig.
Minor	Bonding	High	-.27	.08	1,2	.00	2,3	.33
Delinquency		Low	-.10	.43	1,3	.26	2,4	.07
					1,4	.00	3,4	.02

			Delinquent Peer Involvement		Significance of Group Differences*			
	Conventional		Low	High	Group	Sig.	Group	Sig.
Marijuana	Bonding	High	-.40	.07	1,2	.00	2,3	.00
Use		Low	-.46	.78	1,3	.24	2,4	.00
					1,4	.00	3,4	.00

			Delinquent Peer Involvement		Significance of Group Differences*			
	Conventional		Low	High	Group	Sig.	Group	Sig.
Illicit	Bonding	High	-.10	-.18	1,2	.19	2,3	.69
Drug Use		Low	-.16	.42	1,3	.19	2,4	.00
					1,4	.00	3,4	.00

* Significance - As determined by unequal variance t-test. Groups identified by the following scheme.

	Delinquent Peer Involvement			
Conventional	Low	High	Group Sizes	
Bonding High	Grp 1	Grp 2	1 - 257	
Low	Grp 3	Grp 4	2 - 162	
			3 - 77	
			4 - 170	

TABLE 7.5

**Means of Adjusted Delinquency and Drug Use Category Scale Scores
for Groups Defined by Levels of Conventional Bonding and
Involvement with Delinquent Peers: 1977 to 1978 for
Total NYS Sample**

			Delinquent Peer Involvement		Significance of Group Differences*			
	Conventional		Low	High	Group	Sig.	Group	Sig.
General	Bonding	High	-.77	.18	1,2	.00	2,3	.00
Delinquency		Low	-.58	1.13	1,3	.27	2,4	.01
					1,4	.00	3,4	.00

			Delinquent Peer Involvement		Significance of Group Differences*			
	Conventional		Low	High	Group	Sig.	Group	Sig.
Index	Bonding	High	-.08	-.08	1,2	.99	2,3	.69
Offenses		Low	-.10	.20	1,3	.48	2,4	.00
					1,4	.00	3,4	.00

			Delinquent Peer Involvement		Significance of Group Differences*			
	Conventional		Low	High	Group	Sig.	Group	Sig.
Minor	Bonding	High	-.30	.18	1,2	.00	2,3	.00
Delinquency		Low	-.31	.46	1,3	.96	2,4	.04
					1,4	.00	3,4	.00

			Delinquent Peer Involvement		Significance of Group Differences*			
	Conventional		Low	High	Group	Sig.	Group	Sig.
Marijuana	Bonding	High	-.18	.20	1,2	.00	2,3	.00
Use		Low	-.33	.58	1,3	.22	2,4	.01
					1,4	.00	3,4	.00

			Delinquent Peer Involvement		Significance of Group Differences*			
	Conventional		Low	High	Group	Sig.	Group	Sig.
Illicit	Bonding	High	-.18	-.07	1,2	.04	2,3	.12
Drug Use		Low	-.18	.40	1,3	.96	2,4	.00
					1,4	.00	3,4	.00

* Significance - As determined by unequal variance t-test. Groups identified
by the following scheme.

		Delinquent Peer Involvement			
		Low	High	Group Sizes	
Conventional		Low	High	1 - 498	
Bonding	High	Grp 1	Grp 2	2 - 231	
	Low	Grp 3	Grp 4	3 - 221	
				4 - 447	

TABLE 7.6

Means of Adjusted Delinquency and Drug Use Category Scale Scores for Groups Defined by Levels of Conventional Bonding and Involvement with Delinquent Peers: 1977 to 1978, Males

			Delinquent Peer Involvement		Significance of Group Differences*			
	Conventional		Low	High	Group	Sig.	Group	Sig.
General	Bonding	High	-1.00	.41	1,2	.00	2,3	.00
Delinquency		Low	-.83	1.33	1,3	.48	2,4	.11
					1,4	.00	3,4	.00

			Delinquent Peer Involvement		Significance of Group Differences*			
	Conventional		Low	High	Group	Sig.	Group	Sig.
Index	Bonding	High	-.13	-.05	1,2	.35	2,3	.20
Offenses		Low	-.15	.23	1,3	.48	2,4	.04
					1,4	.00	3,4	.00

			Delinquent Peer Involvement		Significance of Group Differences*			
	Conventional		Low	High	Group	Sig.	Group	Sig.
Minor	Bonding	High	-.42	.25	1,2	.00	2,3	.00
Delinquency		Low	-.36	.57	1,3	.59	2,4	.13
					1,4	.00	3,4	.00

			Delinquent Peer Involvement		Significance of Group Differences*			
	Conventional		Low	High	Group	Sig.	Group	Sig.
Marijuana	Bonding	High	-.52	.45	1,2	.00	2,3	.00
Use		Low	-.37	.56	1,3	.21	2,4	.58
					1,4	.00	3,4	.00

			Delinquent Peer Involvement		Significance of Group Differences*			
	Conventional		Low	High	Group	Sig.	Group	Sig.
Illicit	Bonding	High	-.23	-.06	1,2	.05	2,3	.14
Drug Use		Low	-.22	.44	1,3	.91	2,4	.00
					1,4	.00	3,4	.00

* Significance - As determined by unequal variance t-test. Groups identified by the following scheme.

		Delinquent Peer Involvement		Group Sizes		
Conventional		Low	High	1	-	227
Bonding	High	Grp 1	Grp 2	2	-	89
	Low	Grp 3	Grp 4	3	-	144
				4	-	268

TABLE 7.7

Means of Adjusted Delinquency and Drug Use Category Scale Scores for Groups Defined by Levels of Conventional Bonding and Involvement with Delinquent Peers: 1977 to 1978, Females

			Delinquent Peer Involvement		Significance of Group Differences*			
	Conventional		Low	High	Group	Sig.	Group	Sig.
General	Bonding	High	−.50	.18	1,2	.00	2,3	.01
Delinquency		Low	−.64	.93	1,3	.53	2,4	.05
					1,4	.00	3,4	.00

			Delinquent Peer Involvement		Significance of Group Differences*			
	Conventional		Low	High	Group	Sig.	Group	Sig.
Index	Bonding	High	−.04	−.07	1,2	.36	2,3	.94
Offenses		Low	−.06	.14	1,3	.34	2,4	.00
					1,4	.00	3,4	.00

			Delinquent Peer Involvement		Significance of Group Differences*			
	Conventional		Low	High	Group	Sig.	Group	Sig.
Minor	Bonding	High	−.20	.21	1,2	.00	2,3	.00
Delinquency		Low	−.33	.32	1,3	.24	2,4	.56
					1,4	.00	3,4	.00

			Delinquent Peer Involvement		Significance of Group Differences*			
	Conventional		Low	High	Group	Sig.	Group	Sig.
Marijuana	Bonding	High	−.38	.14	1,2	.00	2,3	.00
Use		Low	−.31	.63	1,3	.46	2,4	.01
					1,4	.00	3,4	.00

			Delinquent Peer Involvement		Significance of Group Differences*			
	Conventional		Low	High	Group	Sig.	Group	Sig.
Illicit	Bonding	High	−.14	−.13	1,2	.02	2,3	.03
Drug use		Low	−.13	.28	1,3	.50	2,4	.09
					1,4	.00	3,4	.00

* Significance - As determined by unequal variance t-test. Groups identified by the following scheme.

		Delinquent Peer Involvement		Group Sizes		
Conventional		Low	High	1	-	268
Bonding	High	Grp 1	Grp 2	2	-	146
	Low	Grp 3	Grp 4	3	-	82
				4	-	175

tional bonding generally has the next highest level of involvement in delinquency and drug use, while the high delinquent
peer involvement and low conventional bonding group always
has the highest level of involvement in these behaviors.
Whenever there are statistical differences between the groups,
the rank order of the different groups by their mean values is the
order indicated above. This is the order that we specified in
Chapter 3 as that specified by the integrated theory.

Of particular importance to the theoretical development
presented earlier is the comparison of the two groups with high
bonding to delinquent peers because it was expected that the
presence of strong conventional bonds might partially amelio-
rate the influence of delinquent peers on delinquent behavior.
The expected difference is observed in all comparisons, although
the differences in means are not always statistically significant
(nonsignificant for 9 out of 30 tests; $p \leq .05$). Although the lack
of statistical significance implies that in some instances (particularly marijuana use for males in 1978 and minor delinquency
for females in 1978) levels of conventional bonding may not
have a differential effect on the delinquency of youths who have
a high involvement with delinquent peers, the consistency with
which the mean differences exceed or approach conventional
significance levels across sexes for both delinquency and drug
use measures suggests that high conventional bonding does act
as an insulator against the effects of bonding to delinquent
peers.

Because the data presented in Tables 7.2 to 7.7 are based on
categorical or rate responses to the self-reported delinquency
items, the actual magnitude of group differences in terms of the
number of delinquent behaviors is difficult to ascertain. To
illustrate group differences in numbers of delinquent acts, the
procedure for obtaining adjusted delinquency scores described
previously was applied to the SRD open-end frequency scores
and the means of the delinquent peer involvement by conventional bonding groups were recalculated. These means are
presented in Tables 7.8 and 7.9.

Individuals in the two groups that have lower involvement
with delinquent peers have, on the average, a substantially
lower number of offenses than would be expected on the basis

TABLE 7.8

Means of Adjusted Total Delinquency Frequency Scale Scores for Groups Defined by Levels of Conventional Bonding and Involvement with Delinquent Peers: 1976 to 1977

Total Sample			Delinquent Peer Involvement		Significance of Group Differences*			
	Conventional		Low	High	Group	Sig.	Group	Sig.
General	Bonding	High	-12.43	-2.86	1,2	.00	2,3	.00
Delinquency		Low	-11.09	23.13	1,3	.43	2,4	.00
					1,4	.00	3,4	.00

Males			Delinquent Peer Involvement		Significance of Group Differences*			
	Conventional		Low	High	Group	Sig.	Group	Sig.
General	Bonding	High	-17.33	-5.22	1,2	.00	2,3	.06
Delinquency		Low	-14.85	29.48	1,3	.50	2,4	.00
					1,4	.00	3,4	.00

Females			Delinquent Peer Involvement		Significance of Group Differences*			
	Conventional		Low	High	Group	Sig.	Group	Sig.
General	Bonding	High	-6.46	.99	1,2	.01	2,3	.26
Delinquency		Low	-3.57	12.24	1,3	.31	2,4	.03
					1,4	.00	3,4	.00

* Significance - As determined by unequal variance t-test. Groups identified by the following scheme.

Conventional		Delinquent Peer Involvement Low	High
Bonding	High	Grp 1	Grp 2
	Low	Grp 3	Grp 4

of their prior delinquency. The group with high delinquent peer involvement and high conventional bonding has, on the average, a somewhat lower number of offenses than would be expected or is close to the expected number. Most striking, however, is the large number of offenses commited by the high delinquent peer involvement and low conventional bonding group. This number is substantially greater than that expected on the basis of their prior delinquency. Among members of this group,

TABLE 7.9

Means of Adjusted Total Delinquency Frequency Scale Scores for Groups Defined by Levels of Conventional Bonding and Involvement with Delinquent Peers: 1977 to 1978

Total Sample			Delinquent Peer Involvement		Significance of Group Differences*			
	Conventional		Low	High	Group	Sig.	Group	Sig.
General	Bonding	High	-8.63	-4.68	1,2	.17	2,3	.47
Delinquency		Low	-6.78	18.38	1,3	.35	2,4	.00
					1,4	.00	3,4	.00

Males			Delinquent Peer Involvement		Significance of Group Differences*			
	Conventional		Low	High	Group	Sig.	Group	Sig.
General	Bonding	High	-11.95	-3.95	1,2	.22	2,3	.35
Delinquency		Low	-9.88	21.32	1,3	.51	2,4	.01
					1,4	.00	3,4	.00

Females			Delinquent Peer Involvement		Significance of Group Differences*			
	Conventional		Low	High	Group	Sig.	Group	Sig.
General	Bonding	High	-4.98	-.81	1,2	.16	2,3	.21
Delinquency		Low	-5.18	11.97	1,3	.92	2,4	.05
					1,4	.00	3,4	.00

* Significance - As determined by unequal variance t-test. Groups identified by the following scheme.

			Delinquent Peer Involvement	
	Conventional		Low	High
	Bonding	High	Grp 1	Grp 2
		Low	Grp 3	Grp 4

males report more than 20 offenses over that expected and females more than 10 offenses over their expected scores. In comparison, other groups show either a decrease or a very small increase over the expected frequency. These data most clearly indicate the conditional effect of conventional bonding on the delinquent peer involvement-delinquent behavior relationship. On the basis of these frequency data, involvement with delinquent peers appears to be a salient factor in increasing delinquent involvement only in the presence of low bonding to conventional groups and activities.

SUMMARY

The findings reviewed above indicate that persons characterized by low bonding to delinquent peers are less delinquent than would be expected on the basis of their previous delinquency and that the level of conventional bonding has little effect on these persons' delinquency. Persons who are strongly bonded to delinquent peers are more delinquent than those who are not, and the volume of their delinquency is dependent on their level of conventional bonding. Low conventional bonding in conjunction with high bonding to delinquent peers leads to a substantially higher frequency of delinquent behavior.

N O T E

1. Descriptions of the basic K-means clustering algorithm can be found in Hartigan (1975) and Anderberg (1973). The actual method used is a modification of an algorithm described by Sparks (1973) that removes the influence of outlying points and merges clusters whose centroids are separated by a distance less than a given threshold. To provide equal weighting to each of the four variables used in the clustering process, standardized scores were used.

8

Conclusions

In this final chapter we will review the explanatory power and predictive efficiency of the integrated model and compare the results of this test to other multivariate tests of theoretical models. The implications of the findings for each causal linkage postulated in the model will then be discussed and several modifications to the model proposed. Finally we will briefly discuss the policy and treatment implications of these findings.

EXPLANATORY POWER AND
PREDICTIVE EFFICIENCY

The results of this test indicate that the explanatory power of the integrated model is quite high relative to the multivariate tests of pure and mixed explanatory models reviewed in Chapters 1 to 4. When the general delinquency measure (SRD) was the criterion measure, the model accounted for 52-58 percent of the variance in delinquency (total sample). When the criterion measure involved serious delinquent acts, the level of explained variance was smaller, but still substantial (32 to 36 percent). For marijuana use, the model accounted for 59 percent of the variance (both initial test and replication); and for hard drug use it explained 29-34 percent of the variance. The integrated model thus accounts for a major portion of the variance in general delinquency and marijuana use and a substantial portion of the variance in the more serious forms of these behaviors.

None of the predictive (longitudinal) studies reviewed earlier accounted for more than 50 percent of the variance in either delinquency or marijuana use (actual range was 18 to 44 percent). One exception to this generalization involved the study by Jessor and Jessor (1977) that achieved a level of explanation that was similar to that in this study for both a general deviance measure and a marijuana use measure.[1] The predictive power of the model for serious forms of delinquency and drug use is also quite high compared to earlier longitudinal studies (e.g., see Kandel et al., 1978).

In comparison, several cross-sectional tests of mixed theoretical models have achieved levels of explanation as high or higher than those reported here (e.g., Patterson and Dishion, 1984; Meier and Johnson, 1977; Figueira-McDonough et al., 1981; Clayton and Voss, 1981). The predictive power achieved is thus quite good relative to other longitudinal studies, but is not exceptionally high when compared with multivariate cross-sectional tests of other mixed models. In most cases, these other models are mixed social learning and social control models. Several cross-sectional tests of a pure social learning model also report comparable levels of predictive power for marijuana use (Akers et al., 1979, Akers and Cochran, 1983).

There is also some evidence that the integration of control and learning theories resulted in some predictive efficiency; i.e., an increase in predictive power over that attributable to either individual theory. Although this conclusion hinges upon the particular conceptualization of theories presented here and this particular set of measures, it certainly appears that the integrated model improved upon a pure control model. Had we ignored the normative orientation of peers and used a simple measure of bonding to peers, the level of explained variance would have been substantially less. For example, using the involvement with peers measure as a predictor in the path analysis without weighting it by the normative orientation of peers, the level of explained variance would have been 13 percent (SRD2, total sample). Using other measures of general peer bonding (e.g., importance of peers or influence of peers) would not have improved substantially upon this level of predictive power.[2] If the normative orientation of peers is ignored, bonding to peers contributes little to the explanation of delinquency.

The comparison of the integrated model to a pure social learning model is more problematic. As noted earlier in Chapter 4, it might be possible to formulate a social learning model that would include all of the predictors used in the test of the integrated theory because social learning theory would include both restraints (punishments) and motivation (rewards) as causes of delinquency. However, it is not clear that a social learning model would have predicted a conditional relationship between conventional bonding (restraints) and deviant bonding (rewards). The claim for predictive efficiency relative to a pure social learning model rests on the observed interaction between conventional bonding and deviant bonding measures. The findings clearly support the interaction claim. The predictive efficiency resulting from adding the interaction effects to the linear regression model was relatively small (a 4 percent relative increase in explained variance), but statistically significant and substantively important.

In sum, the explanatory power of the integrated model is quite good, given the level of prediction currently reported in the delinquency and drug use literature. Further, the consistency in the initial and replication findings increases our confidence in these estimates of the model's explanatory power. And finally, the evidence suggests that the integrated model has greater predictive power than any of the pure theoretical models included in the integration.

The fact that the model tested included prior delinquency/ drug use as a predictor variable raises the question of how much of the predictive power of the model is due to this measure as compared to the more theoretical measures in the model. To address this question, a separate test was made in which prior delinquency was left out of the model. For the total sample predicting SRD in 1977, the reduced model included the same paths as reported earlier, but the overall level of explained variance dropped to 42 percent. Removal of the prior delinquency measure thus resulted in a 19 percent decrease in explained variance (from 52 to 42 percent). This level of explained variance in general delinquency is still better than that reported in earlier predictive studies (except Jessor and Jessor, 1977) and close to that reported by the Jessors in their field test.

A comparison of the path coefficients for prior delinquency and involvement with delinquent peers reveals that involvement with delinquent peers was the stronger predictor in the initial analysis. This generalization held for all criterion measures and both males and females. In the replication analysis, this pattern was reversed and prior delinquency became the stronger predictor. This change was primarily the result of an increase in the prior delinquency-delinquency relationship rather than a decrease in the involvement with delinquent peers-delinquency relationship. The latter correlation was relatively stable over the two analysis periods (.59 and .64), whereas the former correlation increased from .58 in the initial analysis to .71 in the replication analysis. Overall, it appears that the integrated model has good predictive power and that the relationships between theoretical variables in the model are relatively stable.

EVALUATION OF SPECIFIC CAUSAL LINKAGES IN THE MODEL

The findings clearly support the claim that it is the integrated path that accounts for virtually all of the explained variance in delinquency and drug use. The only measure having a direct effect on delinquency and drug use was bonding to deviant peers, and the effects of strain and conventional bonding were almost totally indirect, mediated by the level of bonding to deviant peers. Neither strain nor conventional bonding had any substantial direct effect upon subsequent delinquency or drug use. The consistency of this finding was remarkable; it held for all measures of delinquency and drug use, for both males and females, and for the initial and replication studies. A comparison of the full models in each of these analyses (see Appendix

B) indicates that in 24 of the 30 tests made, strain and conventional bonding accounted for no more than 1 percent of the variance in the criterion measure; in five cases these measures accounted for 2 percent of the variance; and in one case (females, marijuana use, replication test) they accounted for an additional 3 percent in explained variance. There is little support here for either a pure strain or a pure control model.

Given the potential significance of this finding, it is important to ask whether this test constituted a fair and reasonable test of the effects of strain and conventional bonding upon subsequent delinquency and drug use. This question may be approached in several ways. First, it may be argued that the measures of conventional bonding and strain are unusually weak or poor measures of these theoretical variables and that our failure to find any evidence of direct effects for these measures can be attributed to their unreliability or questionable validity. We do not believe there is any tangible evidence to support this argument. The reliabilities of these measures as reflected by conventional measures of internal consistency are within the acceptable range for social attitude measures (Helmstadter, 1970); we believe they have reasonably good face validity; and the zero-order concurrent and lagged correlations between these measures and the delinquency/drug use measures are as high or higher than those typically reported for other strain and conventional bonding measures (see Table 8.1). The predictive validity of these measures appears as good or better than many other measures of these constructs used in earlier studies (see, for example, Hirschi, 1969; Jensen, 1972; Hindelang, 1973; Krohn and Massey, 1980; Elliott and Voss, 1974; Aultman, 1979; Meade and Mardsen, 1981; Cernkovich, 1978; Segrave and Hastad, 1983; Eve, 1978; Thompson et al., 1982; Akers and Cochran, 1983; Linden, 1978; Wiatrowski et al., 1981; and Johnstone, 1981). Although we acknowledge that our modeling analysis did not consider measurement error, there is no direct evidence that our measures of strain or conventional bonding were particularly weak predictor measures as compared to others used in prior studies.

TABLE 8.1
Concurrent and Lagged (one-year) Correlations Between Strain and Conventional Bonding Predictors and Delinquency/Drug Use Criterion Measures: Initial Test 1976-1977

Predictors	Delinquency/Drug Use Criterion Measures									
	SRD1	SRD2	Index1	Index2	Minor1	Minor2	Marij1	Marij2	HardDrug1	HardDrug2
Strain										
Home Strain 1	.21	.14	.12	.09	.17	.13	.19	.18	.13	.12
School Strain 1	.16	.13	.13	.08	.13	.11	.10	.11	.07	.05
Conventional Bonding										
Family Involvement 2	-.19	-.21	-.12	-.12	-.16	-.21	-.22	-.30	-.15	-.19
Family Normlessness 1	-.31	-.23	-.15	-.15	-.28	-.23	-.25	-.27	-.12	-.15
School Involvement 2	-.22	-.22	-.12	-.12	-.18	-.20	-.18	-.20	-.09	-.13
School Normlessness 1	-.33	-.25	-.26	-.17	-.29	-.21	-.25	-.28	-.12	-.14

Second, it may be argued that the four specific measures of conventional bonding used in the test of the integrated model do not adequately represent the relevant dimensions of bonding. Our conceptualization of social controls focused upon two general dimensions; internal controls reflecting personal beliefs in the moral validity of conventional norms and external controls reflecting involvement in and commitment to conventional groups, institutions, and activities. The specific measures used in the path analysis were selected to be representative of these two dimensions in each of two institutions: The family and school. Although we cannot assess the effect of including other dimensions of conventional bonding or other institutional settings that are not represented in our set of measures, we can assess the extent to which the reduced set used in the analysis captures the explained variance of the total set of conventional bonding predictors available. In a multiple regression analysis, the total set of five family bonding measures accounted for 13 percent of the variance in SRD2; the total set of five school bonding measures accounted for 16 percent of the variance in SRD2. The two family bonding predictors and the two school bonding predictors selected for use in the path analysis each account for approximately 80 percent of the explained variance attributed to their respective sets of measures. The conventional bonding measures used in the path analysis do appear to capture most of the explanatory power of the total set of family and school bonding measures available in this study.

Third, it might be argued that the relative strength of conventional bonding and deviant bonding measures is influenced by the temporal ordering of the measures in the path model and that the use of clearly antecedent measures of all predictor variables would have resulted in significant direct effects for conventional bonding and strain measures. Both of the strain measures and two of the four conventional bonding measures were clearly antecedent to the criterion measures in the path analysis. However, the other two conventional bonding measures (i.e., involvement measures) and the two deviant bonding measures were concurrent with the criterion measures. A path model in which all predictor measures were based upon Wave 1 data and the criterion measure (SRD) was based upon Wave 2 data was examined.[3] The results of this analysis again revealed a strong direct effect of involvement with delinquent peers and no direct effects of either strain or conventional bonding measures. The level of explained variance was lower, but the analysis essentially replicated the earlier findings.

In sum there is no evidence that the strain and conventional bonding measures used in this analysis were unreliable, invalid, or unrepresentative indicators of their respective theoretical constructs. Nor is there any evidence that the failure to find significant direct effects for strain and conventional bonding measures in the original path analysis was the result of using several concurrent predictor measures. Taken together, these findings provide good support for the claims that bonding to delinquent peers is the most proximate cause of delinquency and drug use and that the effects of strain and conventional bonding are indirect and mediated by the level of bonding to delinquent peers.

Not all of the causal paths in the model were supported. Although the path analyses indicated that conventional bonding influenced deviant bonding, there was no evidence that strain led directly to involvement with delinquent peers. This finding supports Kornhauser's (1978) claim that the effects of strain on delinquency are entirely mediated by weak conventional bonds; i.e., there was no evidence of direct effects of strain on either deviant bonding or delinquency/drug use. The only influence of strain was to attenuate conventional bonds. Home strain did contribute to a declining involvement with the family, a declining involvement at school, and increased school normlessness. School strain contributed only to weak bonding at school (both involvement and normlessness). All of these effects of strain were very weak.

The path analysis did indicate that weak conventional bonds contributed to an increasing involvement with delinquent peers. The three conventional bonding measures accounted for 18 to 23 percent of the variation in deviant bonding. Although this level of explained variance is not high it is substantial and supports the integrated model's claim that weak conventional bonds have an indirect effect upon delinquency. The strongest predictor of involvement with delinquent peers was school normlessness.

With the exception of the strain-deviant bonding relationship, the path analysis supported all the causal relationships specified in the integrated model. The level of explanation for bonding to deviant peers, the major intervening variable in the model, is clearly not very high, but we acknowledged at the outset that the model was not fully identified relative to this variable. In our suggested modifications of the model, we will attempt to increase the level of explanation for this critical intervening variable in the model by including additional variables.

THE INTERACTION BETWEEN CONVENTIONAL AND DELINQUENT BONDING

The analyses focusing upon the postulated interaction between conventional and deviant bonding were uniformly supportive. In the regression analyses, controlling for level of conventional bonding clearly specified the relationship between involvement with delinquent peers and delinquent behavior, increasing the strength of the relationship under the condition of weak bonds and decreasing the relationship under the condition of strong bonds. Further, there was a significant but small (2 percent) net increase in the level of explained variance when interaction terms were included in the regression model. The effect was more dramatic when the sample was partitioned into groups with high and low scores on each variable and adjusted subgroup means on delinquency and drug use measures were compared. The only subgroup with positive gains in delinquency and drug use over time was the subgroup characterized by low conventional and high deviant bonding. The other subgroups reported either negative gains or essentially "no change" over time. This pattern of findings was observed for all delinquency/drug use measures, for both males and females, and in the initial and replication analyses. Further, the relative increase in delinquency reported by the subgroup with weak conventional and strong deviant bonds was quite dramatic. Compared to expected rates (based upon prior delinquency scores), males in this subgroup reported an average of nearly 30 more offenses than expected in 1977 and over 20 more offenses than expected in 1978. Females reported an average of approximately 12 more offenses than expected in each year. The fact that the interaction appears stronger in the typological analysis than the linear modeling analysis suggests that the interaction may be a nonlinear one.

It is of interest to note that those youths who were most marginal to all social groups; i.e., those with weak bonds to the family and school and *no* involvement with friends (either delinquent or nondelinquent) reported gains in delinquency that were close to zero (e.g., $M = 2.15$, SRD2 frequency scores, total sample).[4] This finding has important implications for the integrated theory. From a pure control perspective, this subgroup should have reported the highest positive gains in delinquency and drug use. The fact that this group reports substantially less involvement in delinquency than the group with low conventional and high delinquent peer bonding is thus inconsistent with a pure control perspective; it is consistent with the integrated theory. It also supports the claim that delinquent behavior is reinforced or rewarded by delinquent peer groups. If involvement with delinquent peers involves only an absence of peer restraints on delinquency (Hirschi and Gottfredson, 1980), then those with no friends and those with delinquent friends should report similar levels of involvement in delinquency because both are characterized as having no peer restraints on delinquency. The fact that those bonded to delinquent peers report substantially higher levels of delinquency suggests that more than an absence of restraints is involved in the association with delinquent peers. This evidence is admittedly indirect, but it is consistent with the more direct evidence presented by Cohen (1977), Kandel (1978), Andrews and Kandel (1979), Akers et al. (1979), and Akers and Cochran (1983).

There is no evidence here that weak conventional bonding leads to delinquency or drug use in the absence of involvement with delinquent peers. On the other hand, bonding to delinquent peers does appear to increase the risks of delinquency and drug use for all youths. Among those involved with delinquent peers, the risk of increased involvement in delinquency and drug use is substantially greater for youths with weak as compared to strong conventional bonds. However, bonding to delinquent peers led to some increase in delinquency for all youths, whether their conventional bonding was weak or strong. The total set of findings appears consistent with the position that bonding to delinquent peers is a "necessary cause" of delinquency and drug use. There is almost no risk of increasing delinquency if one has no involvement with delinquent peers regardless of his or her level of conventional bonding or strain. If one is involved with delinquent peers, then there is some probability of an involvement in delinquency; this probability varies with the strength of his or her bonds to conventional groups, norms, and activities. Strong conventional bonds thus decrease the likelihood that one will become involved with delinquent peers; and in the event one is involved with delinquent peers, it appears to at least partially insulate him or her from the pro-delinquent influences of the delinquent group.

PROPOSED MODIFICATIONS TO
THE INTEGRATED MODEL

In light of the above findings, several modifications are proposed for the integrated theoretical model. These modifications are indicated in the revised integrated model presented in Figure 8.1. First, there is no evidence to support the causal relationship between strain and bonding to delinquent peers, and this causal path is eliminated from the model. As noted in our earlier review, the evidence for this indirect effect from prior research was weak at best (Meade and Marsden, 1981; Elliott and Voss, 1974). This change essentially relegates

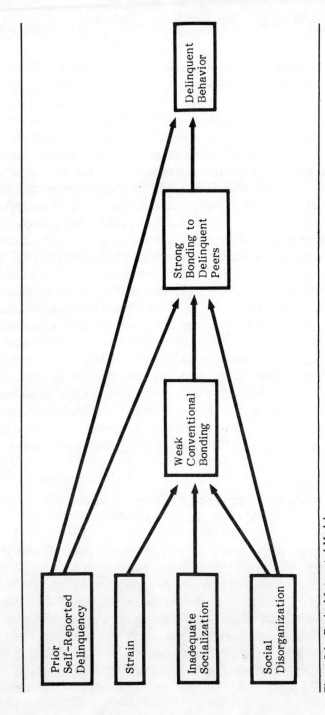

Figure 8.1: Revised Integrated Model

strain to an antecedent cause of weak conventional bonding with no direct causal influence on any of the other variables in the model.

Second, two new paths are proposed to increase the explained variance in bonding to delinquent peers. We noted earlier in our review of studies addressing the two causal orderings of delinquent peers and delinquency that the evidence supports a reciprocal causal relationship between these variables. This reciprocal relationship can be incorporated into the integrated model by including a causal path from prior delinquency to involvement with delinquent peers (see Figure 8.1). We expect that prior delinquency will contribute significantly to the explained variance in bonding to delinquent peers.

We have also included a causal path from social disorganization to delinquent bonding. We believe there is empirical justification for the position that the adolescent peer group is often the only stable social organization in areas characterized as socially disorganized, and that the adolescent groups in these areas frequently have a delinquent orientation (Thrasher, 1927; Shaw and McKay, 1942; Kornhauser, 1978; Short and Strodtbeck, 1965; Yablonsky, 1962; Kobrin, 1951; Johnstone, 1983). In part, the effect of social disorganization should be mediated by weak conventional bonding because the conventional social organizations in these areas are (by definition) poorly integrated, unstable, and ineffective. But at an individual level, some persons living in these areas may not be characterized as having weak conventional bonds, and their reasons for joining delinquent peer groups may be unrelated to their conventional bonding and more a function of the limited availability of peer groups with a conventional orientation. In any event, we will consider this possible causal linkage in the next test of the integrated model.

These two modifications should greatly increase the explained variance in delinquent bonding. However, neither of these proposed modifications will affect the model's explanatory power for delinquency or drug use because bonding to delinquent peers and prior delinquency/drug use remain as the only two direct causes of delinquency and drug use in the revised model. We may expect some increased explanatory power for delinquency with new or improved measures of the predictor and criterion variables. In any case, the results of this initial test of an integrated theoretical model are promising and demonstrate the utility of using more complex, mixed theoretical models in explaining delinquency and drug use.

Finally, it should be noted that the results presented in this book are based on large group data (total sample, males, females). Conceivably there is a typology of youths based on social, demographic, and psychological variables such that the efficacy of the intermix of variables in predicting delinquent behavior is different within different subtypes. Clearly the use of the integrated model to explain the delinquent behavior of a particular individual would be inappropriate. The model does, however, provide some guidance in selecting variables to be examined in providing such an explanation.

IMPLICATIONS FOR TREATMENT
AND PRACTICE

The results of this theoretical test highlight the critical role that adolescent friends play in the production of delinquent behavior. Those youths who are involved with pro-social friends have a very low risk for delinquency; those involved with delinquent friends have a high risk. Although strong bonds to the family and/or school do serve to diminish the pro-delinquent influences of delinquent companions, they do not totally insulate youths from these influences. These findings have obvious implications for delinquency prevention efforts and treatment programs.

Delinquency is embedded in the adolescent peer group context. However, even a cursory review of current prevention and treatment strategies reveals that the peer friendship network has been all but ignored as a specific target for intervention. Even worse, many treatment programs actually facilitate the development of delinquent peer groups, providing increased exposure to a relatively homogeneous group of delinquent peers in the treatment setting and common activities and social identities that serve to strengthen the bonds between those in treatment.

It is particularly ironic that those few treatment approaches that claim to target adolescent peer groups and/or use "group processes" to facilitate individual reform (e.g., gang street worker programs, Positive Peer Culture, and Guided Group Interaction) may actually be contributing to the development, maintenance, and enhancement of delinquent friendship cliques.[5] A key implication of our findings is that normal peer group processes facilitate delinquent as well as conventional behavior; and because these treatment groups rarely include any non-delinquent youth, it is unreasonable to expect that a group of serious chronic offenders will somehow generate a pro-social set of values and group norms by interacting with one another. If a delinquent was placed in a predominantly pro-social peer group it would not be unreasonable to expect group processes to modify his or her beliefs, values, and behavior in the pro-social direction; we would also expect a pro-social person in a predominantly delinquent peer group to modify his or her beliefs and behavior in a delinquent direction. But those who expect a homogeneous group of delinquent youths to reject their current values and beliefs and replace them with a pro-social set of beliefs and values by encouraging and facilitating interpersonal communication and group processes are seriously underestimating the power and influence of the group to reinforce the preexisting delinquent values and beliefs of group members.

Group interactions are not restricted to the treatment setting. Indeed, the treatment setting may be a relatively insignificant context for the evolution of group norms, and what is said by individual group members in formal treatment sessions may have little relevance for group-supported beliefs and behavior outside of that context. There is evidence that the group reinforcements for delinquent behavior in institutional settings is frequently at a nonverbal level of communication (Beuhler et al., 1966). It may even be normative to "play the game" while in formal treatment sessions as a type of "con" that facilitates institutional adjustment or early release from a court-ordered program.

In any case, the results of this study raise serious questions about encouraging group interaction and bonding among delinquent youths as a delinquency control strategy. Although such a strategy is consistent with a pure control perspective that views *any* increase in bonding to peers as a reduction in the risk of delinquency, the findings from this study clearly refute such a position. The normative orientation of the group to which one is bonded is critical to understanding the effect of that bonding upon delinquency.

Increased bonding to delinquent peers is probably an inevitable by-product of incarceration, but it need not be a necessary consequence of all treatment or prevention efforts. Although there may be some circumstances in which it is profitable or advisable to facilitate the interaction of delinquent youths, in general it seems advisable to attempt to minimize it. In contrast, an effort should be made to integrate potentially high-risk youth into conventional peer groups. Ideally, treatment programs should be housed in neutral community settings (like recreational centers or schools) and involve large numbers of pro-social peers in the treatment process. The St. Louis Experiment is one example of this approach that appears highly successful (Feldman et al., 1983). If it is impracticable to achieve this type of integration as a part of treatment, at least the treatment strategy can minimize the opportunities for bonding to deviant peers.

The failure to consider peer group processes extends to our conventional institutional contexts as well. The tracking systems in our schools probably facilitate the formation and maintenance of delinquent peer groups. The practice of placing all troublesome youth in particular classes enhances the likelihood of their developing friendships and working out collective delinquent responses to their home and school situations. Obviously this was not the intent of tracking, but it appears to be a latent function of "ability grouping" (which is frequently based upon deportment rather than ability). A strategy of dispersing troublesome youth as much as possible across teachers and classrooms would structurally minimize the opportunities for the formation of delinquent peer groups in this setting.

Parents have good reason to be concerned about their adolescent children's friends. Although this study and others demonstrate that strong bonding to parents and the school reduces the likelihood of involvement with delinquent peers, this relationship is not exceptionally strong. In this study, over one-third of those classified as having strong conventional bonds were also classified as having above average levels of involvement with delinquent peers (see Table 7.2). Such youths are still at some risk for delinquency although the risk is significantly lower than that for youths who are involved with delinquent peers and have weak bonds to family and school. Although parental control over children's friendship choices is clearly diminished during adolescence, parents should continue to monitor their children's activities and be aware of the kinds of friends who are included in their children's peer network. Parental acquaintance with children's friends and some monitoring or supervision of their activities continue to influence the child's selection of friends during adolescence (Patterson and Dishion, 1984).

Although we view involvement with delinquent peers to be the most critical target for delinquency prevention and treatment efforts, the theory clearly identified other appropriate targets of intervention. Attempts to build stronger bonds to the family, school, church, and other conventional groups and institutions to increase stakes in conformity or to encourage more conventional beliefs are all obvious delinquency prevention strategies that are consistent with the theoretical model. They are particularly appropriate strategies for prevention efforts because they reflect causal conditions that are typically located earlier in the causal sequence leading to delinquency. Our concern is that the peer context has been largely ignored in prior prevention efforts and that interventions involving the family or attempts to modify personal values and belief structures involve greater cost and lower effectiveness than interventions with the peer group (assuming they are both implemented successfully). For prevention, the cost is higher in the sense that it is necessary to treat or intervene in the lives of many youths who have a relatively low risk for delinquency. Weak conventional bonding without involvement with delinquent peers involves a low risk of future delinquency. Other arguments can and should be made in support of treating all youths characterized as having weak conventional bonds, but the reduction in delinquency realized from such an intervention (i.e., the efficiency of the intervention) will be relatively small. In comparison, interventions with delinquent peer groups should have a lower cost and a greater efficiency.

NOTES

1. Jessor and Jessor (1977) report an almost identical level of explained variance for their General Deviance measure using 14 predictor variables (49-56 percent). However, in their field test analysis using six predictor variables that were the best predictors from their conceptual sets of predictors, the level of explained variance was lower (45-46 percent). Their level of explained variance for marijuana use was also very similar to that reported here when using all 14 predictors but substantially lower for the field test (42-46 percent). We consider the field test to represent the test most similar to that presented here, but this study does represent an exception to this generalization.

2. The lagged correlations for peer bonding measures (Wave 1) with delinquent behavior (SRD, Wave 2) for the total sample are as follows: Peer Involvement, .17; Peer Importance, -.02; Peer Influence, .06. The test of a pure control model that included the original conventional bonding measures and the involvement with peers measure did not include SRD1 as a predictor. The resulting R^2 of .13 should thus be compared to an R^2 of .42 for the integrated model without SRD1.

3. SRD1 was excluded as a predictor in the analysis discussed here. Only the theoretical predictor variables were included. The model tested was thus a slightly different model than that tested in Chapter 6, but allows for a comparison of the relative influence of theoretical predictors when all are clearly antecedent to the criterion measure.

4. This involves an analysis similar to that reported earlier in Table 7.8, but for youth who reported having no close friends, and hence no involvement with either delinquent or pro-social friends. As a result, this group of youths were excluded from the analyses reported in Tables 7.2 through 7.9.

5. The results of evaluations of street worker programs with delinquent gangs suggest that the more intensive the service delivered to these groups, the more delinquent they become (Miller, 1962; Klein, 1969, 1971; Carney et al., 1969).

APPENDIX A
Psychometric Properties of NYS Youth Scales

Scale Name	No. Items	Wave 1				Wave 2				Wave 3			
		X̄	SD	A	HR	X̄	SD	A	HR	X̄	SD	A	HR
Family Aspirations	5	22.49	3.18	.70	.32	22.37	3.36	.74	.37	22.15	3.47	.76	.40
Family Achievement	5	18.72	3.96	.72	.34	18.82	4.12	.77	.40	18.79	4.22	.79	.43
Peer Aspirations	4	13.83	3.76	.63	.31	13.71	3.62	.65	.32	14.07	3.59	.65	.32
Peer Achievement	4	14.05	3.36	.69	.36	14.18	3.15	.67	.34	14.39	3.12	.66	.33
Academic Aspirations	5	20.26	3.97	.70	.32	20.14	4.11	.75	.37	19.63	4.31	.78	.41
Academic Achievement	5	17.37	3.70	.69	.31	17.42	3.82	.75	.38	17.24	3.84	.76	.39
Family Social Isolation	5	10.02	2.99	.72	.34	9.78	2.92	.74	.38	9.77	3.09	.79	.44
Peer Social Isolation	5	10.74	2.74	.64	.27	10.32	2.69	.69	.32	9.85	2.61	.74	.37
School Social Isolation	5	11.15	2.95	.64	.27	10.69	2.79	.67	.29	10.47	2.64	.66	.28
Family Normlessness	4	8.88	2.59	.64	.31	8.68	2.51	.66	.33	8.68	2.52	.69	.37
Peer Normlessness	4	8.80	2.41	.60	.28	8.50	2.32	.62	.30	8.41	2.23	.63	.31
School Normlessness	5	11.19	2.85	.60	.23	11.05	2.91	.66	.28	10.98	2.93	.68	.30
Family Labeling (Bad)	4	8.50	2.75	.77	.46	8.20	2.71	.81	.53	8.01	2.66	.83	.56
Peer Labeling (Bad)	4	8.41	2.68	.82	.54	8.35	2.69	.85	.59	8.31	2.74	.86	.62
Teacher Labeling (Bad)	4	8.32	2.65	.85	.59	8.23	2.57	.86	.61	8.27	2.63	.88	.65
Perceived Sanctions-Family	9	41.27	3.42	.84	.37	41.02	3.40	.85	.39	40.69	3.44	.84	.38
Perceived Sanctions-Peers	9	35.92	5.62	.90	.51	35.37	5.37	.89	.49	34.80	5.36	.89	.49
Attitudes Toward Deviance	9	31.32	4.08	.84	.39	30.67	4.34	.85	.42	29.73	4.42	.84	.40
Exposure to Delinquent Peers	10	16.70	5.86	.82	.36	17.14	5.98	.83	.38	17.71	5.99	.83	.37

NOTES: X̄ = Mean Score; SD = Standard Deviation; A = Alpha Reliability Coefficient (Cronbach, 1951); HR = Homogeneity Ratio (Scott, 1960).

APPENDIX B

Path Coefficients, Standard Errors, Residual Paths, and Multiple Correlation Ratio for Full Path Models (separate tabulations for total sample, males, and females for self-reported delinquency, index offenses, minor offenses, marijuana use, and illicit drug use across two replications)

PATH ANALYSIS — Total Sample: Replication 1 — Self-Reported Delinquency

PATH COEFFICIENTS AND STANDARD ERRORS

P(4, 2) = .2896 (+/- .030)
P(4, 3) = .0435 (+/- .039)
P(5, 2) = .2500 (+/- .039)
P(5, 3) = .0421 (+/- .029)
P(6, 2) = .2175 (+/- .029)
P(6, 3) = .1492 (+/- .029)
P(7, 2) = .1332 (+/- .028)
P(7, 3) = .1043 (+/- .028)
P(8, 3) = .0208 (+/- .030)
P(8, 4) = .0509 (+/- .029)
P(8, 5) = .0947 (+/- .036)
P(8, 6) = .1461 (+/- .029)
P(8, 7) = .2247 (+/- .036)
P(9, 2) = .1874 (+/- .029)
P(9, 3) = .0585 (+/- .030)
P(9, 4) = .0116 (+/- .029)
P(9, 5) = .1840 (+/- .036)
P(9, 6) = .1710 (+/- .029)
P(9, 7) = .1764 (+/- .029)
P(10, 1) = .1414 (+/- .029)
P(10, 1) = .3706 (+/- .030)
P(10, 2) = .0225 (+/- .026)
P(10, 3) = .0178 (+/- .025)
P(10, 4) = .0173 (+/- .032)
P(10, 6) = .0487 (+/- .032)
P(10, 7) = .0052 (+/- .026)
P(10, 8) = .4632 (+/- .036)
P(10, 9) = .0268 (+/- .031)

RESIDUAL PATHS AND R-SQUARED

P(4 ,A) = .9522 (.09)
P(5 ,B) = .9546 (.06)
P(7 ,D) = .9814 (.04)
P(8 ,E) = .8855 (.22)
P(9 ,F) = .8772 (.23)
P(10 ,G) = .6876 (.53)

PATH ANALYSIS — Males: Replication 1 — Self-Reported Delinquency

PATH COEFFICIENTS AND STANDARD ERRORS

P(4, 2) = .3166 (+/- .031)
P(4, 3) = .0594 (+/- .029)
P(5, 2) = .2304 (+/- .030)
P(5, 3) = .0468 (+/- .030)
P(6, 2) = .2498 (+/- .030)
P(6, 3) = .1485 (+/- .030)
P(7, 2) = .1847 (+/- .030)
P(7, 3) = .0195 (+/- .031)
P(8, 3) = .0528 (+/- .030)
P(8, 4) = .1174 (+/- .035)
P(8, 5) = .1216 (+/- .029)
P(8, 6) = .1859 (+/- .035)
P(8, 7) = .2247 (+/- .035)
P(9, 2) = .0540 (+/- .031)
P(9, 3) = .0177 (+/- .030)
P(9, 4) = .2248 (+/- .036)
P(9, 5) = .1561 (+/- .029)
P(9, 6) = .1485 (+/- .037)
P(9, 7) = .1250 (+/- .029)
P(10, 1) = .3640 (+/- .030)
P(10, 2) = .0091 (+/- .027)
P(10, 3) = .0148 (+/- .025)
P(10, 4) = .0756 (+/- .024)
P(10, 6) = .0196 (+/- .031)
P(10, 6) = .0508 (+/- .031)
P(10, 7) = .0381 (+/- .025)
P(10, 8) = .5195 (+/- .036)
P(10, 9) = .0255 (+/- .031)

RESIDUAL PATHS AND R-SQUARED

P(4 ,A) = .9394 (.12)
P(5 ,B) = .9760 (.05)
P(7 ,D) = .9425 (.11)
P(8 ,E) = .9690 (.06)
P(8 ,E) = .8975 (.19)
P(9 ,F) = .8819 (.22)
P(10 ,G) = .6722 (.55)

PATH ANALYSIS — Females: Replication 1 — Self-Reported Delinquency

PATH COEFFICIENTS AND STANDARD ERRORS

P(4, 2) = .2675 (+/- .029)
P(4, 3) = .0150 (+/- .028)
P(5, 2) = .2705 (+/- .029)
P(5, 3) = .0381 (+/- .028)
P(6, 2) = .1927 (+/- .029)
P(6, 3) = .1397 (+/- .029)
P(7, 2) = .0004 (+/- .028)
P(7, 3) = .0627 (+/- .029)
P(8, 3) = .0304 (+/- .029)
P(8, 4) = .0507 (+/- .028)
P(8, 5) = .0455 (+/- .037)
P(8, 6) = .1994 (+/- .029)
P(8, 7) = .2786 (+/- .037)
P(9, 2) = .1464 (+/- .029)
P(9, 3) = .0763 (+/- .030)
P(9, 4) = .0111 (+/- .028)
P(9, 5) = .1130 (+/- .037)
P(9, 6) = .2000 (+/- .030)
P(9, 7) = .2191 (+/- .030)
P(9, 7) = .1198 (+/- .029)
P(10, 1) = .3062 (+/- .030)
P(10, 2) = .0334 (+/- .027)
P(10, 3) = .0337 (+/- .026)
P(10, 4) = .0263 (+/- .024)
P(10, 4) = .0601 (+/- .028)
P(10, 6) = .0041 (+/- .035)
P(10, 7) = .0360 (+/- .027)
P(10, 8) = .4257 (+/- .037)
P(10, 9) = .0404 (+/- .032)

RESIDUAL PATHS AND R-SQUARED

P(4 ,A) = .9625 (.07)
P(5 ,B) = .9645 (.07)
P(6 ,C) = .9647 (.07)
P(7 ,D) = .9915 (.02)
P(8 ,E) = .8782 (.23)
P(9 ,F) = .8829 (.22)
P(10 ,G) = .7471 (.44)

Variable List for Full Models

1 - SRD 1
2 - Family Strain 1
3 - School Strain 1
4 - Family Normlessness 2
5 - Family Involvement 2
6 - School Normlessness 1
7 - School Involvement 2
8 - Involvement with Delinquent Peers 2
9 - Attitudes to Deviance 1
10 - SRD 2

PATH ANALYSIS
Total Sample: Replication 1
Index Offenses

PATH COEFFICIENTS AND STANDARD ERRORS

```
P(  4,  2) = .2896  (+/- .030 )
P(  4,  3) = .0435  (+/- .029 )
P(  5,  2) = .2500  (+/- .030 )
P(  5,  3) = .0421  (+/- .029 )
P(  6,  2) = .2175  (+/- .029 )
P(  6,  3) = .1492  (+/- .029 )
P(  7,  2) = .1333  (+/- .029 )
P(  7,  3) = .1042  (+/- .029 )
P(  8,  2) = .0208  (+/- .030 )
P(  8,  3) = .0509  (+/- .029 )
P(  8,  4) = .0947  (+/- .036 )
P(  8,  5) = .1461  (+/- .035 )
P(  8,  6) = .2241  (+/- .029 )
P(  8,  7) = .1874  (+/- .029 )
P(  9,  2) = .0565  (+/- .030 )
P(  9,  3) = .0116  (+/- .029 )
P(  9,  4) = .1840  (+/- .036 )
P(  9,  5) = .1771  (+/- .035 )
P(  9,  6) = .1764  (+/- .036 )
P(  9,  7) = .1414  (+/- .029 )
P(  9,  8) = .3351  (+/- .030 )
P(10,  1) = .0018  (+/- .029 )
P(10,  2) = .0015  (+/- .028 )
P(10,  3) = .4211  (+/- .029 )
P(10,  4) = .0024  (+/- .036 )
P(10,  5) = .0406  (+/- .036 )
P(10,  7) = .0342  (+/- .028 )
P(10,  8) = .4260  (+/- .037 )
P(10,  9) = .0352  (+/- .035 )
```

RESIDUAL PATHS AND R-SQUARED

```
P(  4 ,A) = .9522  (.09 )
P(  5 ,B) = .9706  (.06 )
P(  6 ,C) = .9544  (.09 )
P(  7 ,D) = .9814  (.04 )
P(  8 ,E) = .8855  (.22 )
P(  9 ,F) = .8772  (.23 )
P(10 ,G) = .8239  (.32 )
```

PATH ANALYSIS
Males: Replication 1
Index Offenses

PATH COEFFICIENTS AND STANDARD ERRORS

```
P(  4,  2) = .3166  (+/- .031 )
P(  4,  3) = .0594  (+/- .029 )
P(  5,  2) = .2304  (+/- .030 )
P(  5,  3) = .0468  (+/- .030 )
P(  6,  2) = .2498  (+/- .030 )
P(  6,  3) = .1485  (+/- .030 )
P(  7,  2) = .1647  (+/- .030 )
P(  7,  3) = .1334  (+/- .030 )
P(  8,  2) = .0195  (+/- .031 )
P(  8,  3) = .0528  (+/- .030 )
P(  8,  4) = .1174  (+/- .035 )
P(  8,  6) = .2166  (+/- .029 )
P(  8,  7) = .1855  (+/- .029 )
P(  8,  6) = .1910  (+/- .029 )
P(  9,  2) = .0540  (+/- .031 )
P(  9,  3) = .0177  (+/- .030 )
P(  9,  4) = .2248  (+/- .036 )
P(  9,  5) = .1556  (+/- .029 )
P(  9,  6) = .1487  (+/- .035 )
P(  9,  7) = .1250  (+/- .029 )
P(10,  1) = .3258  (+/- .030 )
P(10,  2) = .0143  (+/- .029 )
P(10,  3) = .0125  (+/- .028 )
P(10,  4) = .4446  (+/- .024 )
P(10,  5) = .0058  (+/- .024 )
P(10,  6) = .0487  (+/- .034 )
P(10,  7) = .0477  (+/- .028 )
P(10,  8) = .4926  (+/- .037 )
P(10,  9) = .0261  (+/- .034 )
```

RESIDUAL PATHS AND R-SQUARED

```
P(  4 ,A) = .9394  (.12 )
P(  5 ,B) = .9425  (.05 )
P(  6 ,C) = .9425  (.11 )
P(  7 ,D) = .9690  (.06 )
P(  8 ,E) = .8975  (.19 )
P(  9 ,F) = .8819  (.22 )
P(10 ,G) = .7898  (.38 )
```

PATH ANALYSIS
Females: Replication 1
Index Offenses

PATH COEFFICIENTS AND STANDARD ERRORS

```
P(  4,  2) = .2675  (+/- .029 )
P(  4,  3) = .0750  (+/- .028 )
P(  5,  2) = .2705  (+/- .029 )
P(  5,  3) = .0381  (+/- .028 )
P(  6,  2) = .1927  (+/- .029 )
P(  6,  3) = .1397  (+/- .029 )
P(  7,  2) = .1004  (+/- .028 )
P(  7,  3) = .0627  (+/- .029 )
P(  8,  2) = .0304  (+/- .029 )
P(  8,  3) = .0507  (+/- .028 )
P(  8,  4) = .0455  (+/- .037 )
P(  8,  5) = .1994  (+/- .030 )
P(  8,  6) = .2786  (+/- .029 )
P(  8,  7) = .1464  (+/- .029 )
P(  9,  2) = .0763  (+/- .030 )
P(  9,  3) = .0111  (+/- .028 )
P(  9,  4) = .1130  (+/- .037 )
P(  9,  5) = .2000  (+/- .030 )
P(  9,  6) = .2131  (+/- .029 )
P(  9,  7) = .1198  (+/- .029 )
P(10,  1) = .2137  (+/- .029 )
P(10,  2) = .0291  (+/- .030 )
P(10,  3) = .0441  (+/- .029 )
P(10,  4) = .0030  (+/- .037 )
P(10,  5) = .0763  (+/- .031 )
P(10,  6) = .0738  (+/- .039 )
P(10,  7) = .0522  (+/- .030 )
P(10,  8) = .2334  (+/- .037 )
P(10,  9) = .0957  (+/- .036 )
```

RESIDUAL PATHS AND R-SQUARED

```
P(  4 ,A) = .9625  (.07 )
P(  5 ,B) = .9645  (.07 )
P(  7 ,D) = .9915  (.02 )
P(  8 ,E) = .8782  (.23 )
P(  9 ,F) = .8829  (.22 )
P(10 ,G) = .9337  (.13 )
```

Variable List for Full Models

```
1 - Index Offense 1              6 - School Normlessness 1
2 - Family Strain 1              7 - School Involvement 2
3 - School Strain 1              8 - Involvement with Delinquent Peers 2
4 - Family Normlessness 2        9 - Attitudes to Deviance 1
5 - Family Involvement 2        10 - Index Offense 2
```

(continued)

APPENDIX B Continued

PATH ANALYSIS
Total Sample: Replication 1
Minor Offenses

PATH COEFFICIENTS AND STANDARD ERRORS

P(4, 2) =	-.2896	(+/- .030)
P(4, 3) =	-.0435	(+/- .029)
P(5, 2) =	.2250	(+/- .029)
P(5, 3) =	.0421	(+/- .029)
P(6, 2) =	-.2175	(+/- .029)
P(6, 3) =	-.1492	(+/- .029)
P(7, 2) =	.1331	(+/- .029)
P(7, 3) =	-.1042	(+/- .029)
P(8, 2) =	.0200	(+/- .029)
P(8, 3) =	.0509	(+/- .029)
P(8, 4) =	-.0947	(+/- .036)
P(8, 5) =	.1461	(+/- .036)
P(8, 6) =	.2247	(+/- .036)
P(8, 7) =	.6874	(+/- .029)
P(9, 2) =	-.0585	(+/- .029)
P(9, 3) =	.0116	(+/- .029)
P(9, 4) =	-.1840	(+/- .036)
P(9, 5) =	.1710	(+/- .036)
P(9, 6) =	.1764	(+/- .036)
P(9, 7) =	.1414	(+/- .029)
P(10, 1) =	.3340	(+/- .028)
P(10, 2) =	.0217	(+/- .028)
P(10, 3) =	-.0220	(+/- .034)
P(10, 4) =	.0368	(+/- .034)
P(10, 5) =	.0480	(+/- .028)
P(10, 6) =	.0748	(+/- .028)
P(10, 7) =	-.0131	(+/- .028)
P(10, 8) =	.3638	(+/- .036)
P(10, 9) =	.0626	(+/- .034)

RESIDUAL PATHS AND R-SQUARED

P(4, A) =	.9522	(.09)
P(5, B) =	.9706	(.06)
P(6, C) =	.9544	(.09)
P(7, D) =	.9810	(.04)
P(8, E) =	.8855	(.22)
P(9, F) =	.8772	(.23)
P(10, G) =	.7758	(.40)

PATH ANALYSIS
Males: Replication 1
Minor Offenses

PATH COEFFICIENTS AND STANDARD ERRORS

P(4, 2) =	-.3166	(+/- .031)
P(4, 3) =	-.0594	(+/- .029)
P(5, 2) =	.2304	(+/- .030)
P(5, 3) =	.0468	(+/- .030)
P(6, 2) =	-.2498	(+/- .030)
P(6, 3) =	-.1485	(+/- .030)
P(7, 2) =	.1647	(+/- .030)
P(7, 3) =	-.1334	(+/- .030)
P(8, 2) =	.0195	(+/- .031)
P(8, 3) =	.0528	(+/- .030)
P(8, 4) =	-.1174	(+/- .035)
P(8, 5) =	.1274	(+/- .035)
P(8, 6) =	.1859	(+/- .035)
P(8, 7) =	.1910	(+/- .029)
P(9, 2) =	-.0540	(+/- .031)
P(9, 3) =	.0177	(+/- .030)
P(9, 4) =	-.2248	(+/- .036)
P(9, 5) =	.1561	(+/- .036)
P(9, 6) =	.1467	(+/- .035)
P(9, 7) =	.1250	(+/- .029)
P(10, 1) =	.3324	(+/- .030)
P(10, 2) =	-.0066	(+/- .029)
P(10, 3) =	.0183	(+/- .028)
P(10, 4) =	-.0298	(+/- .033)
P(10, 5) =	.0406	(+/- .033)
P(10, 6) =	.0689	(+/- .033)
P(10, 7) =	.0177	(+/- .027)
P(10, 8) =	.4734	(+/- .036)
P(10, 9) =	.0572	(+/- .033)

RESIDUAL PATHS AND R-SQUARED

P(4, A) =	.9384	(.12)
P(5, B) =	.9760	(.05)
P(6, C) =	.9425	(.11)
P(7, D) =	.9690	(.06)
P(8, E) =	.8975	(.19)
P(9, F) =	.8819	(.22)
P(10, G) =	.7646	(.42)

PATH ANALYSIS
Females: Replication 1
Minor Offenses

PATH COEFFICIENTS AND STANDARD ERRORS

P(4, 2) =	-.2675	(+/- .029)
P(4, 3) =	-.0150	(+/- .028)
P(5, 2) =	.2705	(+/- .029)
P(5, 3) =	.0381	(+/- .026)
P(6, 2) =	-.1927	(+/- .029)
P(6, 3) =	-.1397	(+/- .029)
P(7, 2) =	.1004	(+/- .028)
P(7, 3) =	-.0627	(+/- .028)
P(8, 2) =	.0304	(+/- .028)
P(8, 3) =	.0507	(+/- .028)
P(8, 4) =	-.0455	(+/- .037)
P(8, 5) =	.1994	(+/- .037)
P(8, 6) =	.2786	(+/- .037)
P(8, 7) =	.1464	(+/- .029)
P(9, 2) =	.0763	(+/- .030)
P(9, 3) =	-.0111	(+/- .028)
P(9, 4) =	-.2100	(+/- .037)
P(9, 5) =	.2191	(+/- .037)
P(9, 6) =	.1198	(+/- .029)
P(9, 7) =	.3353	(+/- .031)
P(10, 1) =	.0414	(+/- .028)
P(10, 2) =	.0276	(+/- .027)
P(10, 3) =	.0419	(+/- .036)
P(10, 4) =	.0741	(+/- .036)
P(10, 5) =	.0676	(+/- .030)
P(10, 6) =	.0511	(+/- .036)
P(10, 7) =	.2672	(+/- .028)
P(10, 8) =	.0736	(+/- .034)

RESIDUAL PATHS AND R-SQUARED

P(4, A) =	.9625	(.07)
P(5, B) =	.9645	(.07)
P(6, C) =	.9647	(.07)
P(7, D) =	.9915	(.02)
P(8, E) =	.8782	(.23)
P(9, F) =	.8629	(.22)
P(10, G) =	.8110	(.34)

Variable List for Full Models

1	– Minor Offense 1		6	– School Normlessness 1
2	– Family Strain 1		7	– School Involvement 2
3	– School Strain 1		8	– Involvement with Delinquent Peers 2
4	– Family Normlessness 2		9	– Attitudes to Deviance 1
5	– Family Involvement 2		10	– Minor Offense 2

PATH ANALYSIS — Total Sample: Replication 1 — Marijuana Use

PATH COEFFICIENTS AND STANDARD ERRORS

Parameter	Coefficient		Std. Error
P(4, 2)	.2896	(+/-	.030)
P(4, 3)	.0435	(+/-	.029)
P(5, 2)	.2500	(+/-	.030)
P(5, 3)	.0421	(+/-	.029)
P(6, 2)	-.2175	(+/-	.029)
P(6, 3)	-.1492	(+/-	.029)
P(7, 2)	-.1331	(+/-	.029)
P(7, 3)	.1042	(+/-	.029)
P(8, 2)	.0508	(+/-	.030)
P(8, 3)	.0509	(+/-	.030)
P(8, 4)	.0947	(+/-	.036)
P(8, 5)	.1461	(+/-	.029)
P(8, 6)	-.2247	(+/-	.036)
P(8, 7)	-.1874	(+/-	.029)
P(9, 2)	.0585	(+/-	.030)
P(9, 3)	.0116	(+/-	.029)
P(9, 4)	.1840	(+/-	.036)
P(9, 5)	.1710	(+/-	.036)
P(9, 6)	.1764	(+/-	.036)
P(9, 7)	.1414	(+/-	.029)
P(10, 2)	-.4660	(+/-	.030)
P(10, 3)	.0170	(+/-	.024)
P(10, 4)	.0082	(+/-	.023)
P(10, 5)	-.0093	(+/-	.030)
P(10, 6)	.0828	(+/-	.024)
P(10, 7)	.0306	(+/-	.030)
P(10, 8)	.0391	(+/-	.024)
P(10, 9)	.3362	(+/-	.032)
P(10, 9)	.1372	(+/-	.030)

RESIDUAL PATHS AND R-SQUARED

Parameter	Value	R²
P(4,A) =	.9522	(.09)
P(5,B) =	.9706	(.06)
P(6,C) =	.9544	(.09)
P(7,D) =	.9421	(.22)
P(8,E) =	.8855	(.22)
P(9,F) =	.8772	(.23)
P(10,G) =	.6243	(.61)

PATH ANALYSIS — Males: Replication 1 — Marijuana Use

PATH COEFFICIENTS AND STANDARD ERRORS

Parameter	Coefficient		Std. Error
P(4, 2)	.3166	(+/-	.031)
P(4, 3)	-.0594	(+/-	.029)
P(5, 2)	.2304	(+/-	.030)
P(5, 3)	.0468	(+/-	.030)
P(6, 2)	-.2498	(+/-	.030)
P(6, 3)	-.1485	(+/-	.030)
P(7, 2)	-.1647	(+/-	.030)
P(7, 3)	.1334	(+/-	.030)
P(8, 2)	.0195	(+/-	.030)
P(8, 3)	.0228	(+/-	.031)
P(8, 4)	.1174	(+/-	.035)
P(8, 5)	.1216	(+/-	.029)
P(8, 6)	-.1859	(+/-	.035)
P(8, 7)	-.1910	(+/-	.029)
P(9, 2)	.0540	(+/-	.030)
P(9, 3)	.0177	(+/-	.030)
P(9, 4)	.1561	(+/-	.036)
P(9, 5)	.1487	(+/-	.035)
P(9, 6)	.1250	(+/-	.029)
P(9, 7)	-.4962	(+/-	.031)
P(10, 2)	.0186	(+/-	.023)
P(10, 3)	.0145	(+/-	.028)
P(10, 4)	-.0883	(+/-	.023)
P(10, 5)	.0442	(+/-	.023)
P(10, 6)	.0286	(+/-	.023)
P(10, 7)	.3097	(+/-	.030)
P(10, 8)	.1432	(+/-	.029)

RESIDUAL PATHS AND R-SQUARED

Parameter	Value	R²
P(4,A) =	.9394	(.12)
P(5,B) =	.9760	(.05)
P(6,C) =	.9425	(.11)
P(7,D) =	.9590	(.06)
P(8,E) =	.8975	(.19)
P(9,F) =	.8819	(.22)
P(10,G) =	.6009	(.64)

PATH ANALYSIS — Females: Replication 1 — Marijuana Use

PATH COEFFICIENTS AND STANDARD ERRORS

Parameter	Coefficient		Std. Error
P(4, 2)	.2675	(+/-	.029)
P(4, 3)	-.0150	(+/-	.028)
P(5, 2)	.2705	(+/-	.029)
P(5, 3)	.0381	(+/-	.028)
P(6, 2)	-.1927	(+/-	.029)
P(6, 3)	-.1397	(+/-	.029)
P(7, 2)	-.1004	(+/-	.028)
P(7, 3)	-.0627	(+/-	.028)
P(8, 2)	.0304	(+/-	.029)
P(8, 3)	.0457	(+/-	.029)
P(8, 4)	-.0455	(+/-	.037)
P(8, 5)	.1994	(+/-	.030)
P(8, 6)	-.2786	(+/-	.037)
P(8, 7)	-.1464	(+/-	.029)
P(9, 2)	.0763	(+/-	.030)
P(9, 3)	.0111	(+/-	.028)
P(9, 4)	.1130	(+/-	.037)
P(9, 5)	.2000	(+/-	.030)
P(9, 6)	.2191	(+/-	.037)
P(9, 7)	.1198	(+/-	.029)
P(10, 2)	-.4248	(+/-	.029)
P(10, 3)	.0204	(+/-	.025)
P(10, 4)	.0369	(+/-	.024)
P(10, 5)	-.0470	(+/-	.031)
P(10, 6)	.0687	(+/-	.026)
P(10, 7)	.0507	(+/-	.032)
P(10, 8)	.0405	(+/-	.025)
P(10, 9)	.3797	(+/-	.033)
P(10, 9)	.1185	(+/-	.030)

RESIDUAL PATHS AND R-SQUARED

Parameter	Value	R²
P(4,A) =	.9625	(.07)
P(5,B) =	.9645	(.07)
P(6,C) =	.9647	(.07)
P(7,D) =	.9915	(.02)
P(8,E) =	.8772	(.23)
P(9,F) =	.8829	(.22)
P(10,G) =	.6595	(.57)

Variable List for Full Models

1 - Marijuana Use 1		6 -	School Normlessness 1	
2 - Family Strain 1		7 -	School Involvement 2	
3 - School Strain 1		8 -	Involvement with Delinquent Peers 2	
4 - Family Normlessness 2		9 -	Attitudes to Deviance 1	
5 - Family Involvement 2		10 -	Marijuana Use 2	

(continued)

APPENDIX B Continued

PATH ANALYSIS — Total Sample: Replication 1 — Hard Drug Use

PATH COEFFICIENTS AND STANDARD ERRORS

```
P( 4, 2) =  .2896  (+/- .030)
P( 4, 3) =  .2535  (+/- .029)
P( 5, 2) =  .2505  (+/- .030)
P( 5, 3) =  .0421  (+/- .029)
P( 6, 2) =  .2175  (+/- .029)
P( 6, 3) =  .1492  (+/- .029)
P( 7, 2) =  .1331  (+/- .029)
P( 7, 3) =  .1042  (+/- .029)
P( 8, 2) =  .0206  (+/- .030)
P( 8, 3) =  .0509  (+/- .029)
P( 8, 4) =  .0947  (+/- .029)
P( 8, 5) =  .1461  (+/- .029)
P( 8, 6) =  .1874  (+/- .036)
P( 8, 7) =  .2247  (+/- .036)
P( 9, 2) =  .0585  (+/- .030)
P( 9, 3) =  .0116  (+/- .029)
P( 9, 4) =  .1840  (+/- .036)
P( 9, 5) =  .1710  (+/- .036)
P( 9, 6) =  .1764  (+/- .029)
P( 9, 7) =  .1414  (+/- .036)
P(10, 1) =  .4358  (+/- .030)
P(10, 2) =  .0048  (+/- .030)
P(10, 3) =  .0190  (+/- .028)
P(10, 4) =  .0068  (+/- .035)
P(10, 5) =  .0258  (+/- .029)
P(10, 6) =  .0258  (+/- .029)
P(10, 7) =  .0000  (+/- .028)
P(10, 8) =  .2517  (+/- .035)
P(10, 9) =  .0509  (+/- .035)
```

RESIDUAL PATHS AND R-SQUARED

```
P( 4 ,A) = .9522  ( .09 )
P( 5 ,B) = .9706  ( .06 )
P( 6 ,C) = .9644  ( .07 )
P( 7 ,D) = .9814  ( .04 )
P( 8 ,E) = .8855  ( .22 )
P( 9 ,F) = .8772  ( .23 )
P(10 ,G) = .8123  ( .34 )
```

PATH ANALYSIS — Males: Replication 1 — Hard Drug Use

PATH COEFFICIENTS AND STANDARD ERRORS

```
P( 4, 2) =  .3166  (+/- .031)
P( 4, 3) =  .0594  (+/- .029)
P( 5, 2) =  .2345  (+/- .030)
P( 5, 3) =  .0468  (+/- .030)
P( 6, 2) =  .2498  (+/- .030)
P( 6, 3) =  .1485  (+/- .030)
P( 7, 2) =  .1647  (+/- .030)
P( 7, 3) =  .0134  (+/- .030)
P( 8, 2) =  .0528  (+/- .030)
P( 8, 3) =  .1174  (+/- .030)
P( 8, 4) =  .1216  (+/- .035)
P( 8, 5) =  .1859  (+/- .035)
P( 8, 6) =  .2926  (+/- .039)
P( 8, 7) =  .0540  (+/- .031)
P( 9, 2) =  .0177  (+/- .030)
P( 9, 3) =  .2248  (+/- .036)
P( 9, 4) =  .1561  (+/- .035)
P( 9, 5) =  .1487  (+/- .035)
P( 9, 6) =  .2556  (+/- .029)
P( 9, 7) =  .1198  (+/- .037)
P(10, 1) =  .5576  (+/- .037)
P(10, 2) =  .0145  (+/- .027)
P(10, 3) =  .0170  (+/- .026)
P(10, 4) =  .0206  (+/- .032)
P(10, 5) =  .0535  (+/- .026)
P(10, 6) =  .0282  (+/- .026)
P(10, 7) =  .0193  (+/- .026)
P(10, 8) =  .2952  (+/- .033)
P(10, 9) =  .0259  (+/- .032)
```

RESIDUAL PATHS AND R-SQUARED

```
P( 4 ,A) = .9394  ( .12 )
P( 5 ,B) = .9760  ( .05 )
P( 6 ,C) = .9425  ( .11 )
P( 7 ,D) = .9911  ( .02 )
P( 8 ,E) = .8975  ( .19 )
P( 9 ,F) = .8819  ( .22 )
P(10 ,G) = .7022  ( .51 )
```

PATH ANALYSIS — Females: Replication 1 — Hard Drug Use

PATH COEFFICIENTS AND STANDARD ERRORS

```
P( 4, 2) =  .2675  (+/- .029)
P( 4, 3) =  .2750  (+/- .028)
P( 5, 2) =  .2705  (+/- .029)
P( 5, 3) =  .0381  (+/- .028)
P( 6, 2) =  .1927  (+/- .029)
P( 6, 3) =  .1397  (+/- .029)
P( 7, 2) =  .1004  (+/- .028)
P( 7, 3) =  .0627  (+/- .028)
P( 8, 2) =  .0304  (+/- .029)
P( 8, 3) =  .0507  (+/- .028)
P( 8, 4) =  .0455  (+/- .037)
P( 8, 5) =  .1994  (+/- .037)
P( 8, 6) =  .2786  (+/- .029)
P( 8, 7) =  .1464  (+/- .027)
P( 9, 2) =  .0763  (+/- .030)
P( 9, 3) =  .0111  (+/- .028)
P( 9, 4) =  .1130  (+/- .037)
P( 9, 5) =  .2000  (+/- .030)
P( 9, 6) =  .2191  (+/- .029)
P(10, 1) =  .2320  (+/- .029)
P(10, 2) =  .0223  (+/- .030)
P(10, 3) =  .0239  (+/- .029)
P(10, 4) =  .0326  (+/- .029)
P(10, 5) =  .0394  (+/- .031)
P(10, 6) =  .0282  (+/- .038)
P(10, 7) =  .0225  (+/- .030)
P(10, 8) =  .1907  (+/- .036)
P(10, 9) =  .0826  (+/- .036)
```

RESIDUAL PATHS AND R-SQUARED

```
P( 4 ,A) = .9625  ( .07 )
P( 5 ,B) = .9645  ( .07 )
P( 6 ,C) = .9647  ( .07 )
P( 7 ,D) = .9915  ( .02 )
P( 8 ,E) = .8782  ( .23 )
P( 9 ,F) = .8829  ( .22 )
P(10 ,G) = .9199  ( .15 )
```

Variable List for Full Models

```
 1 - Hard Drug Use 1             6 - School Normlessness 1
 2 - Family Strain 1             7 - School Involvement 2
 3 - School Strain 1             8 - Involvement with Delinquent Peers 2
 4 - Family Normlessness 2       9 - Attitudes to Deviance 1
 5 - Family Involvement 2       10 - Hard Drug Use 2
```

PATH COEFFICIENTS AND STANDARD ERRORS

$P(4,2) = -.3174 \ (+/- .031)$
$P(4,3) = -.1070 \ (+/- .030)$
$P(5,2) = -.2362 \ (+/- .031)$
$P(5,3) = -.0367 \ (+/- .030)$
$P(6,2) = .1931 \ (+/- .030)$
$P(6,3) = -.2039 \ (+/- .030)$
$P(7,2) = -.1279 \ (+/- .030)$
$P(7,3) = -.1776 \ (+/- .030)$
$P(8,2) = -.0399 \ (+/- .031)$
$P(8,3) = .0423 \ (+/- .030)$
$P(8,4) = .1795 \ (+/- .037)$
$P(8,5) = .1781 \ (+/- .029)$
$P(8,6) = .1690 \ (+/- .036)$
$P(8,7) = .1780 \ (+/- .029)$
$P(9,2) = .0493 \ (+/- .031)$
$P(9,3) = -.1608 \ (+/- .030)$
$P(9,5) = .2344 \ (+/- .036)$
$P(9,6) = .1896 \ (+/- .029)$
$P(9,7) = -.1617 \ (+/- .029)$
$P(10,1) = .5493 \ (+/- .033)$
$P(10,2) = .0085 \ (+/- .026)$
$P(10,4) = -.0165 \ (+/- .025)$
$P(10,5) = -.0350 \ (+/- .031)$
$P(10,6) = -.0193 \ (+/- .024)$
$P(10,7) = -.0286 \ (+/- .030)$
$P(10,8) = .0242 \ (+/- .024)$
$P(10,9) = .0489 \ (+/- .029)$

RESIDUAL PATHS AND R-SQUARED

$P(4,A) = .9282 \ (.14)$
$P(5,B) = .9745 \ (.05)$
$P(6,C) = .9436 \ (.11)$
$P(7,D) = .9667 \ (.07)$
$P(8,E) = .8691 \ (.24)$
$P(9,F) = .8503 \ (.28)$
$P(10,G) = .6418 \ (.59)$

PATH COEFFICIENTS AND STANDARD ERRORS

$P(4,2) = -.3297 \ (+/- .031)$
$P(4,3) = -.0843 \ (+/- .029)$
$P(5,2) = -.2331 \ (+/- .030)$
$P(5,3) = -.0654 \ (+/- .029)$
$P(6,2) = .2070 \ (+/- .030)$
$P(6,3) = -.1826 \ (+/- .030)$
$P(7,2) = -.1467 \ (+/- .030)$
$P(7,3) = -.1422 \ (+/- .030)$
$P(8,2) = -.0463 \ (+/- .031)$
$P(8,3) = .0100 \ (+/- .029)$
$P(8,4) = .1976 \ (+/- .036)$
$P(8,5) = .1912 \ (+/- .028)$
$P(8,6) = .1790 \ (+/- .035)$
$P(8,7) = .1820 \ (+/- .028)$
$P(9,2) = .0560 \ (+/- .030)$
$P(9,3) = -.1401 \ (+/- .029)$
$P(9,5) = .2392 \ (+/- .036)$
$P(9,6) = .1539 \ (+/- .035)$
$P(9,7) = -.1876 \ (+/- .028)$
$P(10,1) = .5468 \ (+/- .033)$
$P(10,2) = .0292 \ (+/- .026)$
$P(10,4) = .0202 \ (+/- .025)$
$P(10,5) = .0168 \ (+/- .035)$
$P(10,6) = -.0313 \ (+/- .025)$
$P(10,7) = .0013 \ (+/- .030)$
$P(10,8) = -.0355 \ (+/- .024)$
$P(10,9) = .0134 \ (+/- .030)$

RESIDUAL PATHS AND R-SQUARED

$P(4,A) = .9297 \ (.14)$
$P(5,B) = .9758 \ (.05)$
$P(6,C) = .9470 \ (.10)$
$P(7,D) = .9713 \ (.06)$
$P(8,E) = .8609 \ (.26)$
$P(9,F) = .8503 \ (.28)$
$P(10,G) = .6488 \ (.58)$

PATH COEFFICIENTS AND STANDARD ERRORS

$P(4,2) = -.3051 \ (+/- .031)$
$P(4,3) = -.1155 \ (+/- .030)$
$P(5,2) = -.2366 \ (+/- .031)$
$P(5,3) = -.0125 \ (+/- .030)$
$P(6,2) = .1833 \ (+/- .031)$
$P(6,3) = -.2030 \ (+/- .031)$
$P(7,2) = -.1110 \ (+/- .030)$
$P(7,3) = -.1925 \ (+/- .031)$
$P(8,2) = -.0367 \ (+/- .031)$
$P(8,3) = .0452 \ (+/- .031)$
$P(8,4) = .1760 \ (+/- .037)$
$P(8,5) = .1659 \ (+/- .029)$
$P(8,6) = .1199 \ (+/- .036)$
$P(8,7) = .1478 \ (+/- .029)$
$P(9,2) = .0476 \ (+/- .031)$
$P(9,3) = -.0068 \ (+/- .030)$
$P(9,4) = -.1712 \ (+/- .037)$
$P(9,5) = -.1377 \ (+/- .036)$
$P(9,6) = .1992 \ (+/- .029)$
$P(9,7) = -.0875 \ (+/- .029)$
$P(10,1) = .4642 \ (+/- .032)$
$P(10,2) = -.0216 \ (+/- .027)$
$P(10,4) = .0016 \ (+/- .027)$
$P(10,5) = .0635 \ (+/- .026)$
$P(10,6) = -.0086 \ (+/- .026)$
$P(10,7) = .0736 \ (+/- .032)$
$P(10,8) = .0134 \ (+/- .025)$
$P(10,9) = .0957 \ (+/- .029)$

RESIDUAL PATHS AND R-SQUARED

$P(4,A) = .9298 \ (.14)$
$P(5,B) = .9728 \ (.05)$
$P(6,C) = .9457 \ (.11)$
$P(7,D) = .9659 \ (.07)$
$P(8,E) = .8902 \ (.21)$
$P(9,F) = .8652 \ (.25)$
$P(10,G) = .6795 \ (.54)$

Variable List for Full Models

1 - SRD 1
2 - Family Strain 1
3 - School Strain 1
4 - Family Normlessness 2
5 - Family Involvement 2
6 - School Normlessness 1
7 - School Involvement 2
8 - Involvement with Delinquent Peers 2
9 - Attitudes to Deviance 1
10 - SRD 2

(continued)

APPENDIX B Continued

PATH ANALYSIS
Total Sample: Replication 2 — Index Offenses

PATH COEFFICIENTS AND STANDARD ERRORS

Path	Coefficient	S.E.
P(4, 2)	-.3174	(+/- .031)
P(4, 3)	-.1070	(+/- .030)
P(5, 2)	-.2362	(+/- .031)
P(5, 3)	-.0367	(+/- .030)
P(6, 2)	-.1937	(+/- .030)
P(6, 3)	-.2039	(+/- .030)
P(7, 2)	-.1279	(+/- .030)
P(7, 3)	-.1776	(+/- .030)
P(8, 3)	-.0059	(+/- .031)
P(8, 4)	.0231	(+/- .030)
P(8, 5)	-.1795	(+/- .037)
P(8, 6)	-.1781	(+/- .036)
P(8, 7)	-.1690	(+/- .029)
P(9, 2)	-.1740	(+/- .031)
P(9, 3)	-.0490	(+/- .030)
P(9, 4)	-.0208	(+/- .030)
P(9, 5)	-.1805	(+/- .036)
P(9, 6)	-.2344	(+/- .029)
P(10, 1)	.1896	(+/- .036)
P(10, 2)	.1617	(+/- .032)
P(10, 3)	.4684	(+/- .029)
P(10, 4)	.0181	(+/- .030)
P(10, 5)	-.0061	(+/- .029)
P(10, 6)	-.0125	(+/- .035)
P(10, 7)	-.0064	(+/- .028)
P(10, 8)	-.0166	(+/- .028)
P(10, 9)	-.2403	(+/- .035)
P(10, 9)	-.0343	(+/- .034)

RESIDUAL PATHS AND R-SQUARED

Path	Coefficient	R²
P(4 ,A)	.9282	(.14)
P(5 ,B)	.9745	(.05)
P(6 ,C)	.9436	(.11)
P(7 ,D)	.9667	(.06)
P(8 ,E)	.8691	(.24)
P(9 ,F)	.8503	(.28)
P(10 ,G)	.8009	(.36)

PATH ANALYSIS
Males: Replication 2 — Index Offenses

PATH COEFFICIENTS AND STANDARD ERRORS

Path	Coefficient	S.E.
P(4, 2)	-.3297	(+/- .031)
P(4, 3)	-.2343	(+/- .030)
P(5, 2)	-.0654	(+/- .030)
P(5, 3)	-.2070	(+/- .030)
P(6, 2)	-.1826	(+/- .030)
P(6, 3)	-.1467	(+/- .030)
P(7, 2)	-.1422	(+/- .030)
P(7, 3)	-.0463	(+/- .031)
P(8, 3)	-.0100	(+/- .029)
P(8, 4)	-.1976	(+/- .036)
P(8, 5)	-.1812	(+/- .028)
P(8, 6)	-.1790	(+/- .028)
P(8, 7)	-.1820	(+/- .028)
P(9, 2)	-.0560	(+/- .030)
P(9, 3)	-.0401	(+/- .029)
P(9, 4)	-.1992	(+/- .036)
P(9, 5)	-.2436	(+/- .029)
P(9, 6)	-.2559	(+/- .035)
P(10, 1)	-.1675	(+/- .028)
P(10, 2)	-.4470	(+/- .032)
P(10, 3)	-.0302	(+/- .030)
P(10, 4)	-.0056	(+/- .028)
P(10, 5)	-.0052	(+/- .035)
P(10, 6)	-.0212	(+/- .035)
P(10, 7)	-.0129	(+/- .028)
P(10, 8)	-.2825	(+/- .037)
P(10, 9)	-.0809	(+/- .035)

RESIDUAL PATHS AND R-SQUARED

Path	Coefficient	R²
P(4 ,A)	.9297	(.14)
P(5 ,B)	.9758	(.05)
P(6 ,C)	.9470	(.10)
P(7 ,D)	.9713	(.06)
P(8 ,E)	.8609	(.26)
P(9 ,F)	.8503	(.28)
P(10 ,G)	.7961	(.37)

PATH ANALYSIS
Females: Replication 2 — Index Offenses

PATH COEFFICIENTS AND STANDARD ERRORS

Path	Coefficient	S.E.
P(4, 2)	-.3051	(+/- .031)
P(4, 3)	-.2155	(+/- .030)
P(5, 2)	-.2366	(+/- .031)
P(5, 3)	-.0125	(+/- .030)
P(6, 2)	-.1833	(+/- .031)
P(6, 3)	-.2030	(+/- .030)
P(7, 2)	-.1110	(+/- .030)
P(7, 3)	-.1925	(+/- .031)
P(8, 3)	-.0387	(+/- .031)
P(8, 4)	.0452	(+/- .031)
P(8, 5)	-.1760	(+/- .037)
P(8, 6)	-.1869	(+/- .036)
P(8, 7)	-.1199	(+/- .036)
P(9, 2)	-.1478	(+/- .031)
P(9, 3)	-.0476	(+/- .030)
P(9, 4)	-.0068	(+/- .037)
P(9, 5)	-.1712	(+/- .037)
P(9, 6)	-.2377	(+/- .029)
P(10, 1)	-.0975	(+/- .036)
P(10, 2)	.2662	(+/- .031)
P(10, 3)	-.0104	(+/- .031)
P(10, 4)	-.0162	(+/- .038)
P(10, 5)	-.0036	(+/- .030)
P(10, 6)	-.0090	(+/- .037)
P(10, 7)	-.0044	(+/- .037)
P(10, 8)	-.0063	(+/- .029)
P(10, 9)	.2681	(+/- .034)
P(10, 9)	.0581	(+/- .034)

RESIDUAL PATHS AND R-SQUARED

Path	Coefficient	R²
P(4 ,A)	.9298	(.14)
P(5 ,B)	.9728	(.05)
P(6 ,C)	.9457	(.04)
P(7 ,D)	.9659	(.07)
P(8 ,E)	.8902	(.21)
P(9 ,F)	.8652	(.25)
P(10 ,G)	.8871	(.21)

Variable List for Full Models

#	Variable	#	Variable
1	Index Offense 1	6	School Normlessness 1
2	Family Strain 1	7	School Involvement 2
3	School Strain 1	8	Involvement with Delinquent Peers 2
4	Family Normlessness 2	9	Attitudes to Deviance 1
5	Family Involvement 2	10	Index Offense 2

PATH ANALYSIS
Total Sample: Replication 2
Minor Offenses

PATH COEFFICIENTS AND STANDARD ERRORS

P(4, 2) = -.3174 (+/- .031)
P(4, 3) = -.1070 (+/- .030)
P(5, 2) = -.2362 (+/- .031)
P(5, 3) = .0367 (+/- .030)
P(6, 2) = -.1937 (+/- .030)
P(6, 3) = -.2039 (+/- .030)
P(7, 2) = -.1279 (+/- .030)
P(7, 3) = -.1776 (+/- .030)
P(8, 2) = -.0399 (+/- .031)
P(8, 3) = .0231 (+/- .030)
P(8, 4) = -.1795 (+/- .037)
P(8, 5) = .1690 (+/- .036)
P(8, 6) = .1780 (+/- .029)
P(8, 7) = .0493 (+/- .031)
P(9, 2) = -.1208 (+/- .030)
P(9, 3) = .0405 (+/- .036)
P(9, 5) = -.2344 (+/- .029)
P(9, 6) = .1896 (+/- .036)
P(9, 7) = .1617 (+/- .029)
P(10, 1) = .4519 (+/- .032)
P(10, 2) = -.0266 (+/- .029)
P(10, 3) = -.0239 (+/- .028)
P(10, 4) = .0049 (+/- .034)
P(10, 5) = -.0060 (+/- .027)
P(10, 6) = .0308 (+/- .034)
P(10, 7) = -.0303 (+/- .027)
P(10, 8) = .0349 (+/- .035)
P(10, 9) = .0897 (+/- .033)

RESIDUAL PATHS AND R-SQUARED

P(4 ,A) = .9282 (.14)
P(5 ,B) = .9745 (.05)
P(6 ,C) = .9436 (.11)
P(7 ,D) = .9667 (.07)
P(8 ,E) = .8691 (.24)
P(9 ,F) = .8503 (.28)
P(10 ,G) = .7445 (.45)

PATH ANALYSIS
Males: Replication 2
Minor Offenses

PATH COEFFICIENTS AND STANDARD ERRORS

P(4, 2) = -.3297 (+/- .031)
P(4, 3) = -.0843 (+/- .029)
P(5, 2) = -.2331 (+/- .030)
P(5, 3) = .0654 (+/- .029)
P(6, 2) = -.2070 (+/- .030)
P(6, 3) = -.1868 (+/- .030)
P(7, 2) = -.1467 (+/- .030)
P(7, 3) = -.1422 (+/- .031)
P(8, 2) = -.0463 (+/- .031)
P(8, 3) = .0100 (+/- .029)
P(8, 4) = -.1976 (+/- .036)
P(8, 5) = .1812 (+/- .035)
P(8, 6) = .1792 (+/- .028)
P(8, 7) = .1820 (+/- .028)
P(9, 2) = .0560 (+/- .030)
P(9, 3) = .0401 (+/- .036)
P(9, 5) = -.1992 (+/- .036)
P(9, 6) = .2436 (+/- .029)
P(9, 7) = .1539 (+/- .035)
P(10, 1) = .1876 (+/- .028)
P(10, 2) = .4502 (+/- .032)
P(10, 3) = -.0017 (+/- .028)
P(10, 4) = -.0239 (+/- .033)
P(10, 5) = .0121 (+/- .037)
P(10, 6) = .0125 (+/- .027)
P(10, 7) = .0495 (+/- .033)
P(10, 8) = .0535 (+/- .027)
P(10, 9) = .3062 (+/- .036)
P(10, 9) = .0441 (+/- .033)

RESIDUAL PATHS AND R-SQUARED

P(4 ,A) = .9297 (.14)
P(5 ,B) = .9756 (.05)
P(6 ,C) = .9470 (.10)
P(7 ,D) = .9713 (.06)
P(8 ,E) = .8609 (.26)
P(9 ,F) = .8503 (.28)
P(10 ,G) = .7371 (.46)

PATH ANALYSIS
Females: Replication 2
Minor Offenses

PATH COEFFICIENTS AND STANDARD ERRORS

P(4, 2) = -.3051 (+/- .035)
P(4, 3) = -.1155 (+/- .030)
P(5, 2) = -.2366 (+/- .031)
P(5, 3) = .0125 (+/- .030)
P(6, 2) = -.1833 (+/- .031)
P(6, 3) = -.2030 (+/- .031)
P(7, 2) = -.1110 (+/- .030)
P(7, 3) = -.1925 (+/- .031)
P(8, 2) = -.0367 (+/- .031)
P(8, 3) = .0452 (+/- .031)
P(8, 4) = -.1760 (+/- .037)
P(8, 5) = .1860 (+/- .037)
P(8, 6) = .1199 (+/- .029)
P(8, 7) = .1478 (+/- .029)
P(9, 2) = .0476 (+/- .031)
P(9, 3) = .0068 (+/- .030)
P(9, 4) = .1712 (+/- .027)
P(9, 5) = -.2377 (+/- .035)
P(9, 6) = .1992 (+/- .036)
P(9, 7) = .0875 (+/- .029)
P(10, 1) = .4616 (+/- .033)
P(10, 2) = .0618 (+/- .029)
P(10, 3) = -.0465 (+/- .029)
P(10, 4) = .0124 (+/- .028)
P(10, 5) = .0008 (+/- .028)
P(10, 6) = .0042 (+/- .034)
P(10, 7) = .0112 (+/- .027)
P(10, 9) = .2050 (+/- .033)
P(10, 9) = .1335 (+/- .032)

RESIDUAL PATHS AND R-SQUARED

P(4 ,A) = .9298 (.14)
P(5 ,B) = .9728 (.05)
P(6 ,C) = .9457 (.11)
P(7 ,D) = .9659 (.07)
P(8 ,E) = .8902 (.21)
P(9 ,F) = .8652 (.25)
P(10 ,G) = .7667 (.41)

Variable List for Full Models

1 - Minor Offense 1
2 - Family Strain 1
3 - School Strain 1
4 - Family Normlessness 2
5 - Family Involvement 2
6 - School Normlessness 1
7 - School Involvement 2
8 - Involvement with Delinquent Peers 2
9 - Attitudes to Deviance 1
10 - Minor Offense 2

(continued)

APPENDIX B Continued

PATH ANALYSIS
Total Sample: Replication 2
Marijuana Use

PATH COEFFICIENTS AND STANDARD ERRORS

```
P( 4, 2) =  .3174 (+/- .031 )
P( 4, 3) = -.1070 (+/- .030 )
P( 5, 2) =  .2362 (+/- .031 )
P( 5, 3) =  .0367 (+/- .030 )
P( 6, 2) =  .1937 (+/- .030 )
P( 6, 3) =  .2039 (+/- .030 )
P( 7, 2) =  .1250 (+/- .030 )
P( 7, 3) = -.1776 (+/- .030 )
P( 8, 2) =  .0399 (+/- .031 )
P( 8, 3) =  .0231 (+/- .030 )
P( 8, 4) =  .1795 (+/- .030 )
P( 8, 5) =  .1769 (+/- .037 )
P( 8, 6) =  .1690 (+/- .036 )
P( 8, 7) =  .1780 (+/- .029 )
P( 9, 2) =  .0493 (+/- .031 )
P( 9, 3) = -.0208 (+/- .030 )
P( 9, 4) =  .1805 (+/- .036 )
P( 9, 5) =  .3449 (+/- .036 )
P( 9, 6) =  .1996 (+/- .036 )
P( 9, 7) =  .1617 (+/- .029 )
P(10, 1) =  .5389 (+/- .032 )
P(10, 2) =  .0072 (+/- .026 )
P(10, 3) = -.0051 (+/- .025 )
P(10, 4) = -.0014 (+/- .024 )
P(10, 5) = -.0342 (+/- .024 )
P(10, 6) =  .0039 (+/- .030 )
P(10, 7) = -.0085 (+/- .024 )
P(10, 8) =  .2311 (+/- .031 )
P(10, 9) =  .1304 (+/- .030 )
```

RESIDUAL PATHS AND R-SQUARED

```
P( 4,A) = .9262 ( .14 )
P( 5,B) = .9734 ( .05 )
P( 6,C) = .9436 ( .11 )
P( 7,D) = .9667 ( .07 )
P( 8,E) = .8691 ( .24 )
P( 9,F) = .8503 ( .28 )
P(10,G) = .6325 ( .60 )
```

PATH ANALYSIS
Males: Replication 2
Marijuana Use

PATH COEFFICIENTS AND STANDARD ERRORS

```
P( 4, 2) =  .3297 (+/- .031 )
P( 4, 3) = -.0643 (+/- .029 )
P( 5, 2) =  .2331 (+/- .030 )
P( 5, 3) =  .0654 (+/- .029 )
P( 6, 2) =  .2070 (+/- .030 )
P( 6, 3) =  .1826 (+/- .030 )
P( 7, 2) =  .1467 (+/- .030 )
P( 7, 3) = -.1422 (+/- .030 )
P( 8, 2) =  .0463 (+/- .031 )
P( 8, 3) =  .0100 (+/- .029 )
P( 8, 4) =  .1976 (+/- .036 )
P( 8, 5) =  .1712 (+/- .036 )
P( 8, 6) =  .1820 (+/- .028 )
P( 8, 7) =  .1820 (+/- .028 )
P( 9, 2) =  .0560 (+/- .030 )
P( 9, 3) =  .0401 (+/- .029 )
P( 9, 4) =  .1992 (+/- .036 )
P( 9, 5) =  .3436 (+/- .035 )
P( 9, 6) =  .1539 (+/- .035 )
P( 9, 7) =  .1876 (+/- .028 )
P(10, 1) =  .5770 (+/- .032 )
P(10, 2) =  .0045 (+/- .025 )
P(10, 3) =  .0047 (+/- .024 )
P(10, 4) =  .0432 (+/- .024 )
P(10, 5) =  .0564 (+/- .023 )
P(10, 6) =  .0543 (+/- .028 )
P(10, 7) = -.0004 (+/- .023 )
P(10, 8) =  .2673 (+/- .031 )
P(10, 9) =  .0875 (+/- .029 )
```

RESIDUAL PATHS AND R-SQUARED

```
P( 4,A) = .9297 ( .14 )
P( 5,B) = .9758 ( .05 )
P( 6,C) = .9470 ( .10 )
P( 7,D) = .9713 ( .06 )
P( 8,E) = .8609 ( .26 )
P( 9,F) = .8503 ( .28 )
P(10,G) = .6055 ( .63 )
```

PATH ANALYSIS
Females: Replication 2
Marijuana Use

PATH COEFFICIENTS AND STANDARD ERRORS

```
P( 4, 2) =  .3051 (+/- .031 )
P( 4, 3) = -.1155 (+/- .030 )
P( 5, 2) = -.2366 (+/- .031 )
P( 5, 3) =  .0125 (+/- .030 )
P( 6, 2) =  .1833 (+/- .031 )
P( 6, 3) =  .2030 (+/- .031 )
P( 7, 2) =  .1110 (+/- .030 )
P( 7, 3) = -.1925 (+/- .031 )
P( 8, 2) =  .0367 (+/- .031 )
P( 8, 3) =  .0452 (+/- .031 )
P( 8, 4) =  .1760 (+/- .037 )
P( 8, 5) =  .1669 (+/- .036 )
P( 8, 6) =  .1199 (+/- .036 )
P( 8, 7) =  .1478 (+/- .029 )
P( 9, 2) =  .0476 (+/- .031 )
P( 9, 3) =  .0068 (+/- .030 )
P( 9, 4) =  .1712 (+/- .037 )
P( 9, 5) =  .2771 (+/- .036 )
P( 9, 6) =  .1992 (+/- .036 )
P( 9, 7) =  .0875 (+/- .029 )
P(10, 1) =  .4646 (+/- .032 )
P(10, 2) =  .0152 (+/- .027 )
P(10, 3) = -.0188 (+/- .026 )
P(10, 4) =  .0025 (+/- .026 )
P(10, 5) = -.0053 (+/- .026 )
P(10, 6) = -.0625 (+/- .032 )
P(10, 7) =  .0188 (+/- .025 )
P(10, 8) =  .1940 (+/- .030 )
P(10, 9) =  .1742 (+/- .030 )
```

RESIDUAL PATHS AND R-SQUARED

```
P( 4,A) = .9298 ( .14 )
P( 5,B) = .9728 ( .05 )
P( 6,C) = .9457 ( .11 )
P( 7,D) = .9659 ( .07 )
P( 8,E) = .8902 ( .21 )
P( 9,F) = .8652 ( .25 )
P(10,G) = .6759 ( .54 )
```

Variable List for Full Models

```
1 - Marijuana Use 1          6 - School Normlessness 1
2 - Family Strain 1          7 - School Involvement 2
3 - School Strain 1          8 - Involvement with Delinquent Peers 2
4 - Family Normlessness 2    9 - Attitudes to Deviance 1
5 - Family Involvement 2    10 - Marijuana Use 2
```

PATH ANALYSIS
Total Sample: Replication 2
Hard Drug Use

PATH COEFFICIENTS AND STANDARD ERRORS

Path	Coefficient	Std Error
P(4, 2) =	-.3174	(+/- .031)
P(4, 3) =	-.1070	(+/- .030)
P(5, 2) =	-.2362	(+/- .031)
P(5, 3) =	-.0367	(+/- .030)
P(6, 2) =	-.1937	(+/- .030)
P(6, 3) =	-.2039	(+/- .030)
P(7, 2) =	-.1776	(+/- .030)
P(7, 3) =	-.1776	(+/- .030)
P(8, 2) =	-.0399	(+/- .031)
P(8, 3) =	.0231	(+/- .030)
P(8, 4) =	-.1795	(+/- .037)
P(8, 5) =	-.1781	(+/- .029)
P(8, 6) =	-.1690	(+/- .029)
P(8, 7) =	-.1780	(+/- .029)
P(9, 2) =	-.0493	(+/- .031)
P(9, 3) =	-.0208	(+/- .030)
P(9, 4) =	-.1805	(+/- .036)
P(9, 5) =	-.1844	(+/- .029)
P(9, 6) =	-.1896	(+/- .036)
P(9, 7) =	-.1617	(+/- .029)
P(10, 1) =	-.4130	(+/- .031)
P(10, 2) =	-.0184	(+/- .030)
P(10, 3) =	-.0116	(+/- .030)
P(10, 4) =	-.0453	(+/- .036)
P(10, 5) =	-.0305	(+/- .029)
P(10, 6) =	-.0571	(+/- .036)
P(10, 7) =	-.0442	(+/- .029)
P(10, 8) =	-.1523	(+/- .035)
P(10, 9) =	-.1032	(+/- .035)

RESIDUAL PATHS AND R-SQUARED

Path	Residual	R²
P(4 ,A) =	.9282	(.14)
P(5 ,B) =	.9745	(.05)
P(6 ,C) =	.9436	(.11)
P(7 ,D) =	.9667	(.07)
P(8 ,E) =	.8691	(.24)
P(9 ,F) =	.8503	(.28)
P(10 ,G) =	.8372	(.30)

PATH ANALYSIS
Males: Replication 2
Hard Drug Use

PATH COEFFICIENTS AND STANDARD ERRORS

Path	Coefficient	Std Error
P(4, 2) =	-.3297	(+/- .031)
P(4, 3) =	-.0843	(+/- .029)
P(5, 2) =	-.2331	(+/- .030)
P(5, 3) =	-.0654	(+/- .029)
P(6, 2) =	-.2070	(+/- .030)
P(6, 3) =	-.1826	(+/- .030)
P(7, 2) =	-.1467	(+/- .030)
P(7, 3) =	-.1422	(+/- .030)
P(8, 2) =	-.0463	(+/- .031)
P(8, 3) =	.0100	(+/- .029)
P(8, 4) =	-.1976	(+/- .036)
P(8, 5) =	-.1812	(+/- .028)
P(8, 6) =	-.1790	(+/- .029)
P(8, 7) =	-.1800	(+/- .030)
P(9, 2) =	-.0560	(+/- .030)
P(9, 3) =	-.0401	(+/- .029)
P(9, 4) =	-.1992	(+/- .036)
P(9, 5) =	-.2436	(+/- .029)
P(9, 6) =	-.1599	(+/- .035)
P(9, 7) =	-.1876	(+/- .028)
P(10, 1) =	-.4763	(+/- .032)
P(10, 2) =	-.0386	(+/- .030)
P(10, 3) =	-.0150	(+/- .028)
P(10, 4) =	-.0754	(+/- .035)
P(10, 5) =	-.0676	(+/- .034)
P(10, 6) =	-.0171	(+/- .028)
P(10, 7) =	-.1200	(+/- .035)
P(10, 8) =	-.1200	(+/- .035)
P(10, 9) =	-.1027	(+/- .035)

RESIDUAL PATHS AND R-SQUARED

Path	Residual	R²
P(4 ,A) =	.9297	(.14)
P(5 ,B) =	.9758	(.05)
P(6 ,C) =	.9470	(.10)
P(7 ,D) =	.9713	(.06)
P(8 ,E) =	.8609	(.26)
P(9 ,F) =	.8503	(.28)
P(10 ,G) =	.8005	(.36)

PATH ANALYSIS
Females: Replication 2
Hard Drug Use

PATH COEFFICIENTS AND STANDARD ERRORS

Path	Coefficient	Std Error
P(4, 2) =	-.3051	(+/- .031)
P(4, 3) =	-.1155	(+/- .030)
P(5, 2) =	-.2366	(+/- .037)
P(5, 3) =	-.0125	(+/- .031)
P(6, 2) =	-.1833	(+/- .031)
P(6, 3) =	-.2030	(+/- .031)
P(7, 2) =	-.1110	(+/- .030)
P(7, 3) =	-.1925	(+/- .031)
P(8, 2) =	-.0387	(+/- .031)
P(8, 3) =	.0452	(+/- .031)
P(8, 4) =	-.1760	(+/- .037)
P(8, 5) =	-.1869	(+/- .029)
P(8, 6) =	-.1199	(+/- .036)
P(8, 7) =	-.1478	(+/- .029)
P(9, 2) =	-.0476	(+/- .031)
P(9, 3) =	-.0068	(+/- .030)
P(9, 4) =	-.1712	(+/- .037)
P(9, 5) =	-.2377	(+/- .029)
P(9, 6) =	-.1992	(+/- .036)
P(9, 7) =	-.2875	(+/- .029)
P(10, 1) =	-.2953	(+/- .037)
P(10, 2) =	-.0190	(+/- .032)
P(10, 3) =	-.0099	(+/- .031)
P(10, 4) =	-.0011	(+/- .038)
P(10, 5) =	-.0313	(+/- .030)
P(10, 6) =	-.0540	(+/- .037)
P(10, 7) =	-.0550	(+/- .030)
P(10, 8) =	-.1948	(+/- .030)
P(10, 9) =	-.1095	(+/- .034)

RESIDUAL PATHS AND R-SQUARED

Path	Residual	R²
P(4 ,A) =	.9298	(.14)
P(5 ,B) =	.9728	(.05)
P(6 ,C) =	.9457	(.11)
P(7 ,D) =	.9609	(.07)
P(8 ,E) =	.8903	(.27)
P(9 ,F) =	.8652	(.25)
P(10 ,G) =	.9008	(.19)

Variable List for Full Models

1 –	Hard Drug Use 1	6 –	School Normlessness 1
2 –	Family Strain 1	7 –	School Involvement 2
3 –	School Strain 1	8 –	Involvement with Delinquent Peers 2
4 –	Family Normlessness 2	9 –	Attitudes to Deviance 1
5 –	Family Involvement 2	10 –	Hard Drug Use 2

REFERENCES

Abelson, H. R., R.Cohen, and D. Schroyer
    1972   "Public attitudes towards marijuana," pp. 856-1119 in Marijuana: A Signal of Misunderstanding. Appendix II, Washington, DC: Government Printing Office.

Akers, R. L.
    1977   Deviant Behavior: A Social Learning Perspective. Belmont, CA: Wadsworth.

Akers, R. L. and J. K. Cochran
    1983   "Adolescent marijuana use: a test of three theories of deviant behavior." Unpublished paper, University of Florida, Gainesville, Florida.

Akers, R. L., M. K. Krohn, L. Lonza-Kaduce, and M. Radosevich
    1979   "Social learning and deviant behavior: a specific test of a general theory." Amer. Soc. Rev. 44: 636-655.

Anderberg, M. R.
    1973   Cluster Analysis for Applications. New York: Academic Press.

Andrews, K. H. and D. B. Kandel
    1979   "Attitude and behavior: a specification of the contingent consistency hypothesis." Amer. Soc. Rev. 44: 298-310.

Aultman, M. G.
    1979   "Delinquency causation: a typological comparison of path models." J. of Criminal Law and Criminology 70: 152-163.

Aultman, M. G. and C. F. Welford
    1979   "Towards an integrated model of delinquency causation: an empirical analysis." Sociology and Social Research 63: 316-327.

Austin, R.
    1977   "Social learning and social control: a comment on Conger." Criminology 15: 111-116.

Bachman, J. G., P. M. O'Malley, and J. Johnston
    1978   "Adolescence to adulthood: change and stability in the lives of young men," in Youth in Transition, Vol. VI. Ann Arbor, MI: Institute for Social Research.

Ball, R. A.
    1966   "An empirical exploration of neutralization theory." Criminologica 4: 22-32.

Bandura, A.
    1969   Principles of Behavior Modification. New York: Holt, Rinehart & Winston.

Bandura, A. and R. H. Walters
  1963   Social Learning and Personality Development. New York: Holt, Rinehart & Winston.
Blalock, H. M., Jr.
  1964   Causal Inferences in Nonexperimental Research. Chapel Hill: Univ. of North Carolina Press.
Braukman, C. J., K. A. Kirigin, and M. M. Wolf
  1980   "Group home treatment research: social learning and social control perspectives," pp. 117-130 in T. Hirschi and M. Gottfredson (eds.) Understanding Crime. Beverly Hills, CA: Sage.
Brennan, T., D. S. Elliott, and B. A. Knowles
  1981   "A descriptive analysis of static types and change patterns, 1976-1978." Project Report No. 15, The Dynamics of Delinquent Behavior: A National Survey. Boulder, CO: Behavioral Research Institute.
Brennan, T., D. Huizinga, and D. S. Elliott
  1978   The Social Psychology of Runaways. Lexington, MA: D. C. Heath.
Briar, S. and I. Piliavin
  1965   "Delinquency, situational inducements, and commitment to conformity." Social Problems 13: 35-45.
Buehler, R. E., G. R. Patterson, and J. M. Furniss
  1966   "The reinforcement of behavior in institutional settings." Behavior Research and Therapy 4: 157-167.
Buffalo, M. D. and J. W. Rogers
  1971   "Behavioral norms, moral norms, and attachment: problems of deviance and conformity." Social Problems 19: 101-113.
Burgess, R. L. and R. L. Akers
  1966   "A differential association—reinforcement theory of criminal behavior." Social Problems 14: 128-147.
Burkett, S. R. and M. White
  1974   "Hellfire and delinquency: another look." J. for the Scientific Study of Religion 13: 455-462.
Carney, F., H. W. Mattick, and J. D. Callaway
  1969   Action on the Streets. New York: Association Press.
Cernkovich, S. A.
  1978   "Value orientations and delinquency involvement." Criminology 15, 4: 443-458.
Clark, J. P. and E. P. Wenninger
  1962   "Socioeconomic class and area correlates of illegal behavior among juveniles." Amer. Soc. Rev. 27: 826-834.
Clayton, R. R. and H. L. Voss
  1981   Young Men and Drugs in Manhattan: A Causal Analysis. Washington, DC: Government Printing Office.
Cloward, R. and L. E. Ohlin
  1960   Delinquency and Opportunity: A Theory of Delinquent Gangs. Glencoe, IL: Free Press.
Cohen, A. K. and J. F. Short, Jr.
  1966   "Juvenile delinquency," pp. 84-135 in R. K. Merton and R. A. Nisbet (eds.) Contemporary Social Problems, 2nd ed. New York: Harcourt Brace Jovanovich.

1976   "Crime and juvenile delinquency," pp. 47-100 in R. K. Merton and R. Nisbet (eds.) Contemporary Social Problems, 2nd ed. New York: Harcourt Brace Jovanovich.

Cohen, J. M.
1977   "Sources of peer group homogeneity." Sociology of Education 50, 4: 227-241.

Conger, R.
1976   "Social control and social learning models of delinquent behavior: a synthesis." Criminology 14, 1: 17-40.
1980   "Juvenile delinquency: behavior restraint or behavior facilitation?" pp. 131-142 in T. Hirschi and M. Gottfredson (eds.) Understanding Crime. Beverly Hills, CA: Sage.

Conklin, J. E.
1971   "Criminal environment and support for the law." Law and Society Rev. 6: 247-259.

Cook, T. D. and D. T. Campbell
1979   Quasi-Experimentation: Design and Analysis Issues for Field Settings. Chicago: Rand McNally.

Cressey, D. R.
1952   "Application and verification of the differential association theory." J. of Criminal Law, Criminology and Police Science 43: 43-52.
1953   Other People's Money. Glencoe, IL: Free Press.

Cronbach, L. J.
1951   "Coefficient alpha and the internal structure of tests." Psychometrika 16: 297-334.

Donovan, J. E. and R. Jessor
1984   "The structure of problem behavior in adolescence and young adulthood." Research Report No. 10, Young Adult Follow-Up Study. Institute of Behavioral Science. Boulder, CO: University of Colorado.

Elliott, D. S.
1961   "Delinquency, opportunity and patterns of orientations." Unpublished Ph.D. dissertation. Seattle: University of Washington.
1962   "Delinquency and perceived opportunity." Sociological Inquiry 32, 2: 216-227.
in press   "The assumption that theories can be combined with increased explanatory power: theoretical integrations." In R. F. Meier (ed.) Theoretical Methods in Criminology. Beverly Hills, CA: Sage.

Elliott, D. S. and R. A. Ageton
1976   "The relationship between drug use and crime among adolescents." Drug Use and Crime: Report of Panel on Drug Use and Criminal Behavior. Research Triangle, NC: Research Triangle Institute.

Elliott, D. S. and S. S. Ageton
1975   The Dynamics of Delinquent Behavior: A National Youth Survey. Grant Application to the National Institute of Mental Health (MH27552). Boulder, CO: Behavioral Research Institute.
1980   "Reconciling race and class differences in self-reported and official estimates of delinquency." Amer. Soc. Rev. 45: 95-110.

Elliott, D. S., S. S. Ageton, and R. J. Canter
1979   "An integrated theoretical perspective on delinquent behavior." J. of Research in Crime and Delinquency 16: 3-27.

Elliott, D. S., S. S. Ageton, D. Huizinga, B. A. Knowles, R. J. Canter
  1983   The Prevalence and Incidence of Delinquent Behavior: 1976-1980. Boulder,
         CO: Behavioral Research Institute.
Elliott, D. S. and D. Huizinga
  1984   "The relationship between delinquent behavior and ADM problems."
         Proceedings of the ADAMHA/OJJDP Research Conference on Juvenile
         Offenders with Serious Drug, Alcohol, and Mental Health Problems.
         Washington, DC: Government Printing Office.
Elliott, D. S., B. A. Knowles, and R. J. Canter
  1981   "The epidemiology of delinquent behavior and drug use among American
         adolescents." Project Report No. 14, A National Youth Survey. Boulder, CO:
         Behavioral Research Institute.
Elliott, D. S. and H. Voss
  1974   Delinquency and Dropout. Lexington, MA: D. C. Heath.
Empey, L. T.
  1978   American Delinquency: Its Meaning and Construction. Homewood, IL:
         Dorsey.
Empey, L. T. and S. G. Lubeck
  1968   "Conformity and deviance in the 'situation of company.'" Amer. Soc. Rev.
         33: 760-774.
  1971   Explaining Delinquency. Lexington, MA: D. C. Heath.
Erickson, M. L. and L. T. Empey
  1965   "Class position, peers and delinquency." Sociology and Social Research
         49: 268-282.
Eve, R.
  1975   "'Adolescent culture,' convenient myth or reality? A comparison of students
         and their teachers." Sociology of Education 48: 152-167.
  1978   "A study of the efficacy and interactions of several theories for explaining
         rebelliousness among high school students." J. of Criminal Law and Crimi-
         nology 49: 115-125.
Farrington, D. P.
  1973   "Self-reports of deviant behavior: predictive and stable?" J. of Criminal
         Law and Criminology 64: 99-110.
Feldman, R. A., T. E. Kaplinger, and J. S. Wodarski
  1983   The St. Louis Conundrum: The Effective Treatment of Anti-Social Youths.
         Englewood Cliffs, NJ: Prentice-Hall.
Ferguson, T.
  1952   The Young Delinquent in His Social Setting. London: Oxford Univ. Press.
Figueira-McDonough, J., W. H. Barton, and R. C. Sarri
  1981   "Normal deviance: gender similarities in adolescent subcultures," pp. 17-
         45 in M. Q. Warren (ed). Comparing Female and Male Offenders. Beverly
         Hills, CA: Sage.
Fredericks, M. A. and M. Molnar
  1969   "Relative occupational anticipations and aspirations of delinquents and
         non-delinquents." J. of Research in Crime and Delinquency 6: 1-7.
Ginsberg, I. J. and J. R. Greenley
  1978   "Competing theories of marijuana use: a longitudinal study." J. of Health
         and Social Behavior 19: 22-34.

Glaser, D.
   1960   "Differential association and criminological prediction." Social Problems
         8: 6-14.
   1979   "A review of crime-causation theory and its application," pp. 203-238 in N.
         Morris and M. Tonry (eds.) Crime and Justice: An Annual Review of
         Research, Vol. I. Chicago: Univ. of Chicago Press.

Glueck, S. and E. T. Glueck
   1950   Unraveling Juvenile Delinquency. Cambridge, MA: Harvard Univ. Press.

Glueck, W. and E. T. Glueck
   1956   Physique and Delinquency. New York: Harper & Row.

Gold, M.
   1963   Status Forces in Delinquent Boys. Ann Arbor: Institute for Social Research,
         University of Michigan.
   1970   Delinquent Behavior in an American City. Belmont, CA: Wadsworth.

Gold, M. and D. J. Reimer
   1975   "Changing patterns of delinquent behavior among Americans 13 to 16 years
         old—1972." Crime and Delinquency Literature 7: 483-517.

Gottfredson, G. D.
   1982   "Role models, bonding and delinquency: an examination of competing
         perspectives." Report No. 331. Baltimore, MD: Center for Social Organi-
         zation of Schools, The Johns Hopkins University.

Gould, L. C.
   1969   "Who defines delinquency: a comparison of self-reported and officially
         reported incidences of delinquency for three racial groups." Social Problems
         16, 3: 325-336.

Hansell, S. and M. D. Wiatrowski
   1981   "Competing conceptions of delinquent peer relations," pp. 93-108 in G. F.
         Jensen (ed.) Sociology of Delinquency: Current Issues. Beverly Hills,
         CA: Sage.

Hardt, R. H. and S. J. Peterson
   1968   "Arrests of self and friends as indicators of delinquency involvement." J. of
         Research in Crime and Delinquency 5: 44-51.

Hartigan, J. A.
   1975   Clustering Algorithms. New York: John Wiley.

Hawkins, D. J. and J. G. Weis
   1980   The Social Development Model: An Integrated Approach to Delinquency
         Prevention. Seattle, WA: Center for Law and Justice, University of Washing-
         ton.

Helmstadter, G. C.
   1970   Research Concepts in Human Behavior. New York: Prentice-Hall.

Hindelang, M. J.
   1970   "The commitment of delinquents to their misdeeds: do delinquents drift?"
         Social Problems 17: 502-509.
   1973   "Causes of delinquency: a partial replication and extension." Social Prob-
         lems 20: 471-487.
   1974   "Moral evaluations of illegal behaviors." Social Problems 21, 3: 370-
         385.

Hindelang, M. J., T. Hirschi, and J. G. Weis
  1975   "Self-reported delinquency: methods and substance." Proposal submitted
          to the National Institute of Mental Health, Department of Health, Educa-
          tion, and Welfare (MH27778).
  1981   Measuring Delinquency. Beverly Hills, CA: Sage.
Hindelang, M. J. and J. Weis
  1972   "The bc-try cluster and factor analysis system: personality and self-reported
          delinquency." Criminology 10: 268-294.
Hirschi, T.
  1969   Causes of Delinquency. Berkeley, CA: Univ. of California Press.
  1979   "Separate and unequal is better." J. of Research in Crime and Delinquency
          16: 34-38.
Hirschi, T. and M. Gottfredson
  1980   "Introduction: the Sutherland tradition in criminology," pp. 7-19 in T.
          Hirschi and M. Gottfredson (eds.) Understanding Crime. Beverly Hills,
          CA: Sage.
Huizinga, D.
  1978   "Description of the national youth sample." Project Report No. 2, A National
          Youth Survey. Boulder, CO: Behavioral Research Institute.
Huizinga, D. and D. S. Elliott
  1981   "A longitudinal study of drug use and delinquency in a national sample of
          youth: an assessment of causal order." Project Report No. 16, A National
          Youth Survey. Boulder, CO: Behavioral Research Institute.
Hyman, H.
  1955   Survey Design and Analysis. New York: Free Press.
Jensen, G. F.
  1972   "Parents, peers and delinquent action: a test of the differential association
          perspective." Amer. J. of Sociology 78: 562-575.
Jensen, G. F. and D. Brownfield
  1983   "Parents and drugs: specifying the consequences of attachment." Criminol-
          ogy 21: 543-554.
Jensen, G. F. and M. L. Erickson
  1978   "Peer commitment and delinquent conduct." Unpublished manuscript.
          Tucson: University of Arizona.
Jensen, G. F. and R. Eve
  1976   "Sex differences in delinquency." Criminology 13: 427-448.
Jensen, G. F. and D. G. Rojek
  1980   Delinquency, A Sociological View. Lexington, MA: D. C. Heath.
Jessor, R.
  1981   "The perceived environment in psychological theory and research," pp.
          297-317 in D. Magnusson (ed.) Toward a Psychology of Situations: An
          Interactional Perspective. Hillsdale, NJ: Erlbaum.
Jessor, R. and S. L. Jessor
  1977   Problem Behavior and Psychosocial Development: A Longitudinal Study of
          Youth. New York: Academic Press.

Jessor, R., T. D. Graves, R. C. Hanson, and S. L. Jessor
  1968 Society, Personality and Deviant Behavior: A Study of a Tri-ethnic Community. New York: Holt, Rinehart & Winston.
Johnson, R. E.
  1979 Juvenile Delinquency and Its Origins. Cambridge, MA: Cambridge Univ. Press.
Johnstone, J.W.C.
  1978 "Social class, social areas and delinquency." Sociology and Social Research 63: 49-72.
  1981 "The family and delinquency: a reappraisal," pp. 25-63 in A. C. Meade (ed.) Youth and Society: Studies of Adolescent Deviance. Chicago: Institute for Juvenile Research.
  1983 "Recruitment to a youth gang." Youth and Society 14: 281-300.
Joreskog, K. G. and D. Sorbom
  1978 LISREL IV: Analysis of Linear Structural Relationships by the Method of Maximum Likelihood. Chicago: National Education Resources, Inc.
Kandel, D. B.
  1973 "Adolescent marijuana use: role of parents and peers." Science 181: 1067-1070.
  1978 "Homophily, selection and socialization in adolescent friendships." Amer. J. of Sociology 84, 2: 427-436.
  1980 "Drug and drinking behavior among youth," in A. Inkeles, J. Gleman, and R. H. Turner (eds.) Annual Review of Sociology, Vol. 6. Palo Alto, CA: Annual Reviews Press.
Kandel, D. B., R. C. Kessler, and R. Z. Margulies
  1978 "Antecedents of adolescent initiation into stages of drug use: a developmental analysis," pp. 73-100 in D. B. Kandel (ed.) Longitudinal Research on Drug Use. New York: John Wiley.
Kelly, D. H. and W. T. Pink
  1973 "School commitment, youth rebellion, and delinquency." Criminology 10: 473-485.
Kessler, R. C.
  1977 "Rethinking the 16-fold table problem." Social Science Research 6: 84-103.
Klein, M. W.
  1969 "Gang cohesiveness, delinquency, and a street work program." J. of Research in Crime and Delinquency 6: 135-166.
  1971 Street Gangs and Street Workers. Englewood Cliffs, NJ: Prentice-Hall.
Knight, B. J. and D. J. West
  1975 "Temporary and continuing delinquency." British J. of Criminology 15, 1: 43-50.
Knowles, B. A.
  1979 "The relationship of adolescent marijuana use to social pressure concerning use." Project Report No. 7, The Dynamics of Delinquent Behavior: A National Survey. Boulder, CO: Behavioral Research Institute.
Kobrin, S.
  1951 "The conflict of values in delinquency areas." Amer. Soc. Rev. 16: 653-661.

Kohn, M.
1959 "Social class and parental values." Amer. J. of Sociology 64: 337-351.
Kornhauser, R. R.
1978 Social Sources of Delinquency. Chicago: Univ. of Chicago Press.
Krohn, M. D.
1974 "An investigation of the effect of parental and peer associations on marijuana use: an empirical test of differential association theory," pp. 75-87 in
M. Riedel and T. P. Thornberry (eds.) Crime and Delinquency: Dimensions
of Deviance. New York: Praeger.
Krohn, M. D. and J. Massey
1980 "Social control and delinquent behavior: an examination of the elements of
the social bond." Soc. Q. 21: 529-543.
Langer, J.
1976 "Dealing culture: the rationalization of the 'hang-loose' ethic." Australian
and New Zealand J. of Sociology 12: 82-100.
Lazarsfield, P. F.
1973 "Mutual relations over time of two attributes: a review and integration of
various approaches," pp. 461-80 in M. Hammer, K. Salzinger, and S.
Sutton (eds.) Psychopathology. New York: John Wiley.
LaGrange, R. L. and H. R. White
1983 "Age differences in delinquency: a test of theory." Paper presented at the
American Society of Criminology Meetings, Denver, CO.
Lerman P.
1968 "Individual values, peer values, and subcultural delinquency." Amer. Soc.
Rev. 33: 219-235.
Linden, R.
1978 "Myths of middle-class delinquency: a test of the generalizability of social
control theory." Youth and Society 9, 4: 407-432.
Linden, E. and J. C. Hackler
1973 "Affective ties and delinquency." Pacific Soc. Rev. 16, 1: 27-46.
Liska, A. E.
1971 "Aspirations, expectations and delinquency: stress and additive models."
Soc. Q. 12, 1: 99-107.
1974 "Comments on Jensen's 'parents, peers, and delinquent action.'" Amer. J.
of Sociology 79: 999-1002.
Luckenbill, D. F. and W. B. Sanders
1977 "Criminal violence," pp. 88-156 in E. Sagarin and F. Montanino (eds.)
Deviants: Voluntary Actors in a Hostile World. Morristown, NJ: General.
Matsueda, R. L.
1982 "Testing control theory and differential association." Amer. Soc. Rev. 47,
4: 489-504.
Matza, D.
1964 Delinquency and Drift. New York: John Wiley.
McCord, W., J. McCord, and I. K. Zola
1959 Origins of Crime. New York: Columbia Univ. Press.
Meade, A. C. and M. E. Marsden
1981 "An integration of classic theories of delinquency," in A. C. Meade (ed.)
Youth and Society: Studies of Adolescent Deviance. Chicago: Institute for
Juvenile Research.

Meier, R. F. and W. T. Johnson
  1977 "Deterrence as social control: the legal and extralegal production of conformity." Amer. Soc. Rev. 42, 2: 292-304.
Merton, R. K.
  1957 Social Theory and Social Structure. Glencoe, IL: Free Press.
Michael, J. A.
  1963 "An empirical evaluation of the culture conflict theory as an explanation of juvenile delinquency." Unpublished paper. New York School of Social Work Research Center, Columbia University.
Miller, W. B.
  1962 "The impact of a 'total community' delinquency control project." Social Problems 10: 168-191.
Minor, W. W.
  1981 "Techniques of neutralization: a reconceptualization and empirical examination." J. of Research in Crime and Delinquency 18, 2: 295-318.
Nettler, G.
  1974 Explaining Crime. New York: McGraw-Hill.
Nygreen, G. T.
  1971 "Interactive path analysis." The American Sociologist 6: 37-43.
Patterson, G. R. and T. J. Dishion
  in press "Contributions of families and peers to delinquency." Research in Criminology.
Poole, E. D. and R. M. Regoli
  1979 "Parental support delinquent friends, and delinquency: a test of interaction effects." J. of Criminal Law and Criminology 70: 188-193.
Reiss, A. J., Jr.
  1951 "Delinquency as the failure of personal and social controls." Amer. Soc. Rev. 16, 2: 196-207.
  1975 "Inappropriate theories and inadequate methods as policy plaques: self-reported delinquency and the law," pp. 211-222 in N. J. Demerath, III, et al. (eds.) Social Policy and Sociology. New York: Academic Press.
Reiss, A. J., Jr., and A. L. Rhodes
  1963 "Status deprivation and delinquent behavior." Soc. Q. 4: 135-149.
  1964 "An empirical test of differential association theory." J. of Research in Crime and Delinquency 1: 13-17.
Robbins, L. N. and G. E. Murphy
  1967 "Drug use in a normal population of young Negro men." Amer. J. of Public Health 57, 9: 1580-1596.
Rossi, P., E. Waite, C. Bose, and R. E. Berk
  1974 "The seriousness of crimes: normative structure and individual differences." Amer. Soc. Rev. 39: 224-237.
Rothstein, E.
  1962 "Attributes related to high social status: a comparison of the perceptions of delinquent and non-delinquent boys." Social Problems 10: 75-83.
Rotter, J. B.
  1954 Social Learning and Clinical Psychology. Englewood Cliffs, NJ: Prentice-Hall.

Schwendinger, H. and J. Schwendinger
  1967   "Delinquent stereotypes of probable victims," pp. 91-105 in M. W. Klein
          (ed.) Juvenile Gangs in Context. Englewood Cliffs, NJ: Prentice-Hall.
Scott, W. A.
  1960   "Measures of test homogeneity." Educ. and Psych. Measurement 20: 751-
          757.
Segrave, J. O. and D. N. Hastad
  1983   "Evaluating structural and control models of delinquency causation: a
          replication and extension." Youth and Society 14: 437-456.
Severy, L. J.
  1970   "Exposure to antisocial behavior." Unpublished Ph.D. dissertation.
          Boulder, CO: University of Colorado.
Shaw, C. R. and H. D. McKay
  1942   Juvenile Delinquency and Urban Areas. Chicago: Univ. of Chicago
          Press.
Short, J. F., Jr.
  1957   "Differential association and delinquency." Social Problems 4: 233-
          239.
  1960   "Differential association as a hypothesis." Social Problems 8: 14-25.
  1964   "Gang delinquency and anomie," pp. 98-127 in M. B. Clinard (ed.) Anomie
          and Deviant Behavior. New York: Free Press.
  1979   "On the etiology of delinquent behavior." J. of Research in Crime and
          Delinquency 16: 28-33.
Short, J. F., Jr., R. Rivera, and R. A. Tennyson
  1965   "Perceived opportunities, gang membership and delinquency." Amer. Soc.
          Rev. 30, 1: 56-67.
Short, J. F., Jr., and F. L. Strodtbeck
  1965   Group Process and Gang Delinquency. Chicago: Univ. of Chicago
          Press.
Simon, W. and J. H. Gagnon
  1976   "The anomie of affluence: a post Mertonian conception." Amer. J. of
          Sociology 82, 2: 356-378.
Simons, R. L., M. G. Miller, and S. M. Aigner
  1980   "Contemporary theories of deviance and female delinquency." J. of
          Research in Crime and Delinquency 17: 42-57.
Sparks, D. N.
  1973   "Euclidean cluster analysis." Applied Statistics 22: 126-130.
Spergel, I.
  1964   Racketville, Slumtown, Haulberg. Chicago: Univ. of Chicago Press.
  1967   "Deviant patterns and opportunities of pre-adolescent Negro boys in three
          Chicago neighborhoods," pp. 38-54 in M. W. Klein (ed.) Juvenile Gangs in
          Context: Theory, Research and Action. Englewood Cliffs, NJ: Prentice-
          Hall.
Stanfield, R. E.
  1966   "The interaction of family variables and gang variables in the etiology of
          delinquency." Social Problems 13: 411-417.
Stinchcombe, A. L.
  1964   Rebellion in a High School. Chicago: Quadrangle Books.

Sutherland, E. H.
1947   Principles of Criminology, 4th ed. Philadelphia, PA: J. B. Lippincott.
Suttles, G.
1968   Social Order of the Slum. Chicago: Univ. of Chicago Press.
Thomas, C. W. and J. M. Hyman
1978   "Compliance theory, control theory and juvenile delinquency," pp. 73-90 in M. D. Krohn and R. L. Akers (eds.) Crime, Law and Sanctions. Beverly Hills, CA: Sage.
Thompson, E. A., K. Smith-DiJulio, and T. Matthews
1982   "Social control theory: evaluating a model for the study of adolescent alcohol and drug use." Youth and Society 13, 3: 303-326.
Thrasher, F. M.
1927   The Gang. Chicago: Univ. of Chicago Press.
Toby, J. and M. Toby
1963   Low School Status as a Predisposing Factor in Subcultural Delinquency. New Brunswick, NJ: Rutgers.
Voss, H. L.
1964   "Differential association and reported delinquent behavior: a replication." Social Problems 12: 78-85.
West, D. J.
1973   Who Becomes Delinquent? London: Heinemann.
West, D. J. and D. P. Farrington
1977   The Delinquent Way of Life. London: Heinemann.
Wheeler, S.
1967   "Delinquency and crime," pp. 201-276 in H. S. Becker (ed.) Social Problems: A Modern Approach. New York: John Wiley.
Wiatrowski, M. D.
1978   "Social control theory and delinquency." Unpublished Ph.D. dissertation. Portland State University.
Wiatrowski, M. D., D. B. Griswold, and M. K. Roberts
1981   "Social control theory and delinquency." Amer. Soc. Rev. 46, 5: 525-541.
Wilson, A. B., T. Hirschi, and G. Elder
1965   Technical Report No. 1: Secondary School Curves. Berkeley, CA: Survey Research Center.
Winfree, L. T., H. E. Theis, and C. T. Griffiths
1981   "Drug use in rural America: a cross-cultural examination of complementary social deviance theories." Youth and Society 12, 4: 465-489.
Witmer, H.
1951   An Experiment in the Prevention of Delinquency: The Cambridge-Sommerville Youth Study. New York: Columbia Univ. Press.
Wootten, B.
1959   Social Science and Social Pathology. London: Allen and Unwin.
Yablonsky, L.
1962   The Violent Gang. New York: Macmillan.
Zigler, E. and I. L. Child
1969   "Socialization," pp. 450-589 in G. Lindzey and E. Aaronson (eds.) Individual in a Social Context. Vol. 3 of the Handbook of Social Psychology. Reading, MA: Addison-Wesley.

ABOUT THE AUTHORS

DELBERT S. ELLIOTT is Director of the Behavioral Research Institute in Boulder, Colorado, and Professor Adjoint in the Department of Sociology, University of Colorado, Boulder, Colorado. He is a co-author of *Delinquency and Dropout* (1974) and *The Social Psychology of Runaways* (1978).

DAVID HUIZINGA is a Senior Research Associate at the Behavioral Research Institute. He is a co-author of *The Social Psychology of Runaways* (1978).

SUZANNE S. AGETON is a Senior Research Associate at the Behavioral Research Institute in Boulder, Colorado. She is the author of *Sexual Assault Among Adolescents* (1983).

All three authors are continuing their work on the longitudinal National Youth Survey, which now includes six waves of data with this national youth panel, covering the period from 1976 to 1983.